Growth and Development

Growth and Development

The Span of Life

TORSTAR BOOKS
New York • Toronto

TORSTAR BOOKS INC.
41 Madison Avenue, Suite 2900
New York, NY 10010

THE HUMAN BODY
Growth and Development:
The Span of Life

Publisher
Bruce Marshall

Art Editor
John Bigg

Creation Coordinator
Harold Bull

Editor
John Clark

Managing Editor
Ruth Binney

Commissioning Editor
Hal Robinson

Contributors
Arthur Boylston, Mike Darton, Loraine
Fergusson, Paulette Pratt

Text Editors
Wendy Allen, Lloyd Lindo, Maria Pal

Researchers
Angela Bone, Jazz Wilson

Picture Researchers
Jan Croot, Dee Robinson

Layout and Visualization
Eric Drewery, Ted McCausland

Artists
Mick Gillah, Aziz Khan, Mick Saunders

Cover Design
Moonink Communications

Cover Art
Paul Giovanopoulous

Production Director
Barry Baker

Production Coordinator
Janice Storr

Business Coordinator
Candy Lee

Planning Assistant
Avril Essery

International Sales
Barbara Anderson

In conjunction with this series Torstar Books offers an electronic digital thermometer which provides accurate body temperature readings in large liquid crystal numbers within 60 seconds.

For more information write to:
Torstar Books Inc.
41 Madison Avenue, Suite 2900
New York, NY 10010

Marshall Editions, an editorial group that specializes in the design and publication of scientific subjects for the general reader, prepared this book. Marshall has written and illustrated standard works on technology, animal behavior, computer usage and the tropical rain forests which are recommended for schools and libraries as well as for popular reference.

Series Consultants

Donald M. Engelman is Professor of Molecular Biophysics and Biochemistry and Professor of Biology at Yale. He has pioneered new methods for understanding cell membranes and ribosomes, and has also worked on the problem of atherosclerosis. He has published widely in professional and lay journals and lectured at many universities and international conferences. He is also involved with National Advisory Groups concerned with Molecular Biology, Cancer, and the operation of National Laboratory Facilities.

Stanley Joel Reiser is Professor of Humanities and Technology in Health Care Center in Houston. He is the author of *Medicine and the Reign of Technology;* coeditor of *Ethics in Medicine: Historical Perspectives and Contemporary Concerns;* and coeditor of the anthology *The Machine at the Bedside.*

Harold C. Slavkin, Professor of Biochemistry at the University of Southern California, directs the Graduate Program in Craniofacial Biology and also serves as Chief of the Laboratory for Developmental Biology in the University's Gerontology Center. His

research on the genetic basis of congenital defects of the head and neck has been widely published.

Lewis Thomas is Chancellor of the Memorial Sloan-Kettering Cancer Center in New York City and University Professor at the State University of New York, Stony Brook. A member of the National Academy of Sciences, Dr. Thomas has served on advisory councils of the National Institutes of Health.

Consultants for Growth and Development

Ralph Lopez is Clinical Associate Professor of Pediatrics at The New York Hospital-Cornell Medical Center and an Associate Attending Pediatrician. He specializes in adolescent medicine, and this interest is reflected in his many articles and contributions to books dealing with various aspects of puberty and adolescence.

Marc Weksler is Wright Professor of Medicine and Director of the Division of Geriatrics and Gerontology at Cornell University Medical College. An immunobiologist, he is recognized for his contributions to the understanding of immune senescence. Dr Weksler has served on advisory committees of the National Institutes of Health and is coeditor of *Practical Geriatric Medicine.*

Lewis Wolpert is Head of the Department of Anatomy and Biology as Applied to Medicine at the Middlesex Hospital Medical School, University of London. His main

interest is in developmental biology, in particular the development of cellular patterns. He is a Fellow of the Royal Society, coeditor of *The Journal of Theoretical Biology* and an Associate Editor of *Developmental Biology.*

Medical Advisor

Arthur Boylston

**Library of Congress
Cataloging in Publication Data**
Main entry under title:

Growth and development.

Includes index.
1. Life cycle, Human. 2. Human growth.
3. Developmental biology. 4. Body, Human.
I. Torstar Books (Firm).
QP83.8.G76   1985   612'.6   85-20882
ISBN 0-920269-22-2 (The Human Body Series)
ISBN 0-920269-68-0 (Growth and Development)
ISBN 0-920269-69-9 (Leatherbound)
ISBN 0-920269-70-2 (School ed.)
20 19 18 17 16 15 14 13 12 11
10   9   8   7   6   5   4   3   2   1
Printed in Belgium

Contents

Introduction:

A Lifetime of Development

The way in which humans grow and develop is a fascinating branch of medical science, and one in which many questions remain unanswered. Although it is possible to chart the changes in size and appearance that occur as the human frame takes shape, how is it that a single fertilized egg is able, in nine short months in the womb, to develop into a perfectly formed new human person?

The miracle of growth and development does not stop at birth but carries on physically, intellectually and emotionally throughout life. Indeed, life is a developmental continuum lasting from conception to death. In every individual the exact course of this continuum is influenced by three major factors — the effects of heredity, the quality of the diet and the nature of the environment.

During the first two years of life outside the womb, physical and mental growth take place more rapidly than at any other stage. With the vital assistance of growth hormone, released into the blood from a gland at the brain's base, internal organs enlarge and take on their "adult" characteristics. As nerves mature and new neural pathways open up for traffic, learning abilities improve also.

Once an infant has passed the significant milestones of walking and talking, steady progress in growth and development are maintained throughout childhood. Then comes the huge growth spurt of puberty, and with it the momentous onset of sexual maturity — with all that is implied for physical and emotional change.

At the end of physical growth — an event that takes place earlier for girls than for boys — there is no need for either intellectual or emotional development to cease, nor for physical fitness to wane. Fit in body and mind, it is much easier to face the physical changes that always take place as the body gets older. Armed with the knowledge that aging is merely part of the span of development, old age can become not merely survivable but enjoyable.

Bridging the generation gap, an adult gently takes a baby's hand. In eighteen years or so, these tiny fingers — like the rest of the baby's body — will grow to adult size. Within only a few years, however, development of the nervous system and muscles will give the growing child the dexterity and coordination to be able to play ball, ride a bicycle and even learn to play a musical instrument.

Chapter 1

Life Before Birth

The moment at which life can be said to have its true beginning is a matter of much debate. But whether it is believed to begin at conception, at the time of birth or, as people in previous centuries believed, when the fetus first moves or "quickens" in the womb, there is absolutely no doubt at all that the story of the growth and development of a single being has its beginning at conception. This is the instant when a sperm from a human male enters and unites with an egg from a human female. The conceptual "act of union" sets in motion a train of events of growth and development that only ends — perhaps more than a century later — when life itself ends.

During the many months and years that usually intervene between life's beginning and its end, the one original fertilized egg cell grows by multiplying millions upon millions of times. As multiplication takes place, so the cells become differentiated into a range of tissues, each designed to do a specific job in the body — from muscles able to contract and produce movement to brain cells capable of providing such human attributes as intellect and memory. All the billions of cells in an adult human being are derived from the original by means of a copying and splitting mechanism. And throughout life cells are constantly dying and being replaced by the same method of cell replication. It is estimated, for example, that every minute a staggering three million dead cells are replaced.

The conception of a new life following sexual intercourse between man and woman usually takes place high in one of the woman's Fallopian tubes which arch out from each side of the womb (uterus) like open-ended pitcher handles. Fertilization brings together two sets of chromosomal material, one half the genetic blueprint from the father, one half the genetic blueprint from the mother. Sperm and egg composition is so programmed that each sperm contains half the total gene complement of the father, each egg half that of the mother. This ensures that when egg and sperm fuse, a full

"Ah Love!" an evocative illustration from the Ruba'iyat of Omar Khayyam, *is a beautiful portrayal of affection and intimacy, feelings which often precede the sexual act that can lead to the creation of a child, the most marvelous symbol of the union of two human beings.*

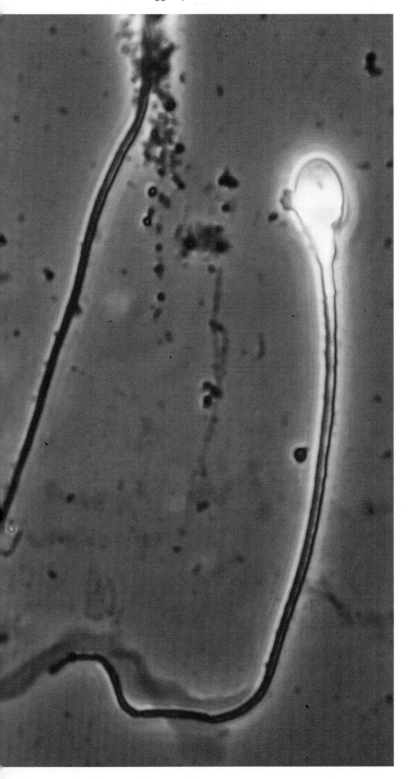

complement of chromosomes exists in the newly fertilized egg. From this a new individual grows, in some forty weeks, from being barely the size of a pinhead to perhaps a bounding eight-pounder. The newborn child emerges with unique genetic make-up, but one which reflects the genetic contribution made by each parent.

It is the genes, life's blueprints, that play the primary role in controlling and determining the course of development, both within the womb and for the span of life after birth. Of course external factors have a vital role to play, but they essentially form the backdrop against which the genes act out their roles. Thus, for example, the mother needs an adequate diet to ensure a proper supply of nutrients to the developing fetus within her. But if the growth program in the genes of the fetus contains a lethal error, there is no diet in the world that the mother can eat to put things right. It is because of the possibility of such errors, some of which damage rather than kill, that modern prenatal care and counseling is continually searching for new methods of detecting genetic abnormality. This may involve genetic counseling before pregnancy is embarked upon, especially if there is known to be an undesirable genetic trait in the family, or the carrying out of a series of tests on mother and embryo in the first stages of pregnancy.

Beginning to Grow

Shortly after conception, while it is still in the Fallopian tube, the fertilized egg undergoes its first copying or mitotic cell division. In this first phase of growth and development, subsequent divisions follow rapidly, yielding progressively smaller cells called blastomeres. By the third day sixteen or so blastomeres have clumped together to form the "morula" (from the Latin for mulberry), and it is this cellular mass which enters the Fallopian tube and then the uterus.

On the fourth day after fertilization the morula, bathed in fluid from the uterine cavity, has already resolved into the "blastocyst," comprising the two segments which are soon to form the major part of the placenta and the embryo itself.

By the end of the first week, the blastocyst is superficially implanted — normally in the endometrium lining the uterus.

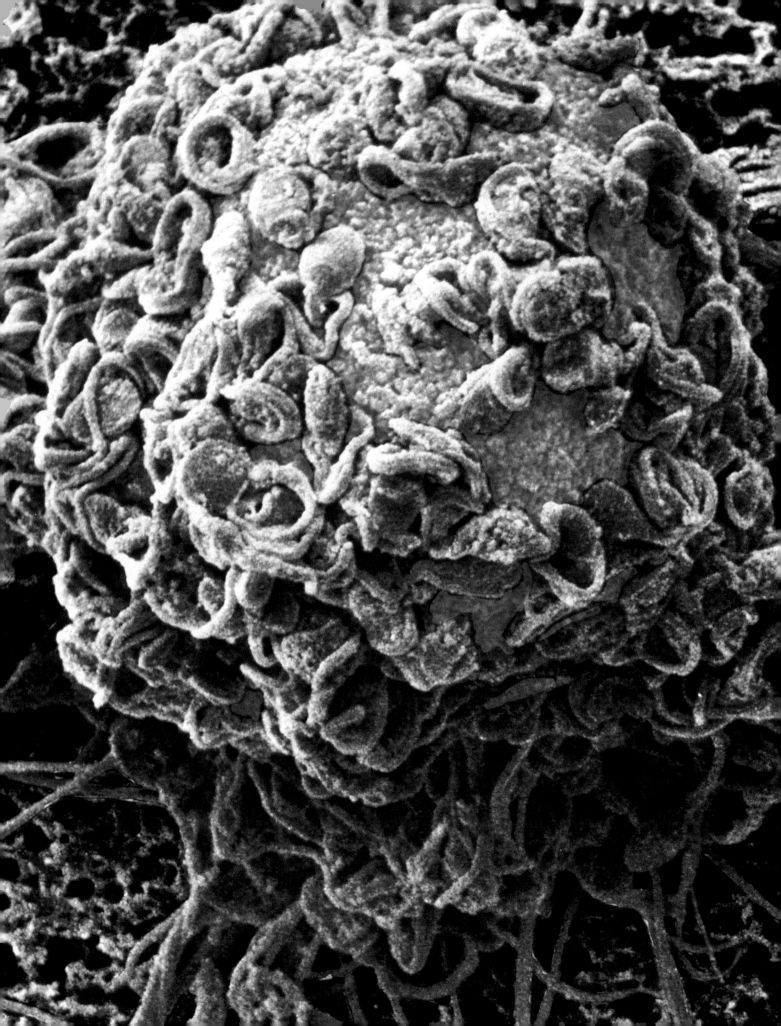

Following fertilization the egg (now known as a zygote) starts to divide, in a process known as cleavage. At the early age of sixty hours the egg has already divided into two cells (far left). This process continues at a

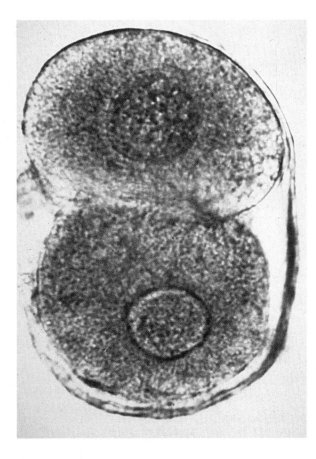

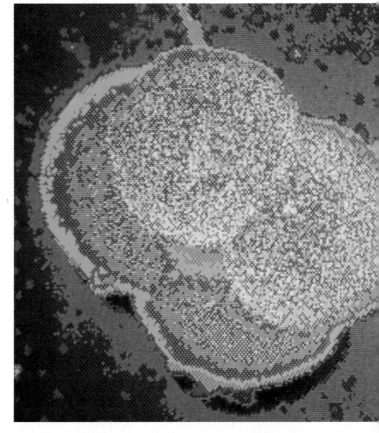

It is usual that by the middle of the second week the blastocyst is completely embedded in the endometrium, drawing oxygen and nutrients from the blood supply to the surrounding maternal tissues. Two structures also develop to support the embryo in the womb. The amnion is the fluid-filled sac which grows around the embryo to envelop it, protecting it from harm; and the body stalk connects the embryo with the uterus.

Pregnancy, then, can be said to be fully established when implantation is complete. By the third week it can be confirmed by pregnancy tests, which detect minute traces of human chorionic gonadotropin (HCG), a hormone produced within the tissues on the outside of the embryo and excreted in the mother's urine.

The early rate of spontaneous abortion from all causes is relatively high. Sixty per cent of fertilized eggs are said to be lost before the first missed period, and 15 per cent of the remaining pregnan-

cies subsequently miscarry. Because more than half of these "discarded" embryos have an abnormal chromosome content, these early losses (comprising what was once termed "pregnancy wastage") may be seen as a natural method of quality control.

The Complexities of Control

The development of a baby is, in every way, truly remarkable. Not least of its near miraculous aspects is the way a single original cell grows and develops into an individual equipped for independent life outside the womb. One of the great mysteries of life, yet to be unraveled, is how the genetic instructions contained in the fertilized egg are translated so that the new human being contains all the different tissues necessary to life, and that all the pieces of the body are put together correctly.

The key to differentiation and development seems to lie in the way the genes work. Fundamen-

rapid rate, with the individual cells, called blastomeres, becoming increasingly smaller, as shown on the computer-enhanced electron micrograph (middle). It takes only three days for sixteen or more such

blastomeres to have formed, when the egg is known as a morula (below right). At this stage it leaves the Fallopian tube and enters the uterus, where it becomes implanted in the endometrium.

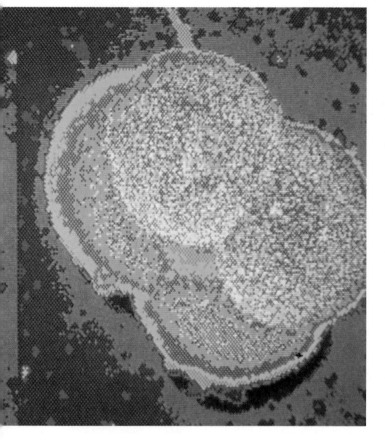

tally, the genes operate by giving out instructions to the cells in which they are contained. These instructions are acted on by the cell, and as a result proteins are manufactured. These proteins are used to build cell structures but also to dictate and control chemical reactions within the cell. As the human egg divides and grows mechanisms come into play whereby different genes are turned on and off at different times. Say, for example, a set of genes programmed to make the proteins specific to muscle cells are turned on, then the cells in which those genes are operating develop into muscle. Similarly, if the genes for making blood proteins are turned on, the cells become blood cells.

Of course the reality is staggeringly more complex than this. In order that one set of genes be turned on, for instance, another set must be repressed or "turned off". And yet more genes act as controllers, dictating which genes should be turned on, and which turned off in any given cell.

Yet further genes give instructions about the intricacies of cell building, and others are programmed to dictate the course of events when the cell divides. Within every cell, chemical messengers — whose manufacture is again dictated by gene action — operate to influence the relationship of a cell with its neighbors.

This concept of neighborliness is vital to development, for it is thought that the way in which the tissues in the developing embryo touch each other influences their behavior and dictates the relationship of the cells one with another. If the touching relationships are wrong, the "pattern pieces" of the human body can end up being put together wrongly or incompletely. The condition of spina bifida results, for instance, from imperfect touching of the parts of the spinal cord, so that a gap is present down part of its length. The result is a child with an imperfectly functioning nervous system, often with paralyzed lower limbs and an

inability to develop control of bladder or rectum —with all that this implies.

Mistakes in the genetic instructions themselves are sometimes responsible for such congenital defects, but external influences can also have a drastic effect on the course of growth and development before birth — and after it, too, of course. Drugs, including alcohol and nicotine, as well as the notorious ones such as thalidomide, can influence the way the genetic message is read, as can X rays and the rubella (German measles) virus.

In a system of such complexity it would be surprising if mistakes and misprints did not occur. One of the most important aims of the continued study of growth and development is to know more about these errors, to detect them as early as possible in pregnancy and to use them for good in understanding more about how the miracle that is the human body is put together.

The earliest test for chromosomal or genetic abnormality is the relatively new technique of chorionic villus sampling, which involves the use of a plastic catheter introduced through the cervix, to remove a few cells from the chorionic sac surrounding the embryo. (Such cells are of course genetically identical with those of the embryo.) Undertaken during the fourth week of gestation, chorionic sampling can reveal genetic anomalies far earlier in pregnancy than does amniocentesis, the more usual test in which fluid is drawn from the amniotic sac and performed on high-risk mothers at fourteen to sixteen weeks. The risks of certain chromosomal abnormalities increase with the age of the mother. The incidence of Down's syndrome (mongolism), for example, in which an extra chromosome is present, increases from fourteen births per ten thousand in mothers under forty years of age to up to a hundred births per ten thousand in mothers over forty.

It is in the third week, however, that the three

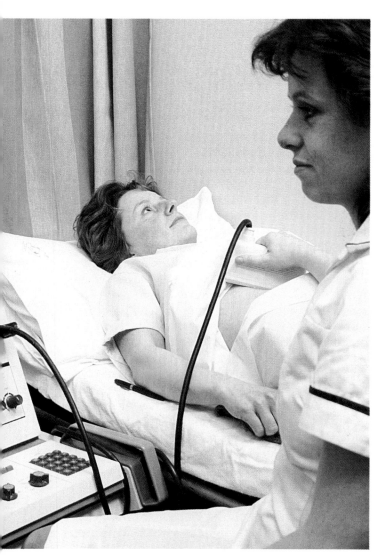

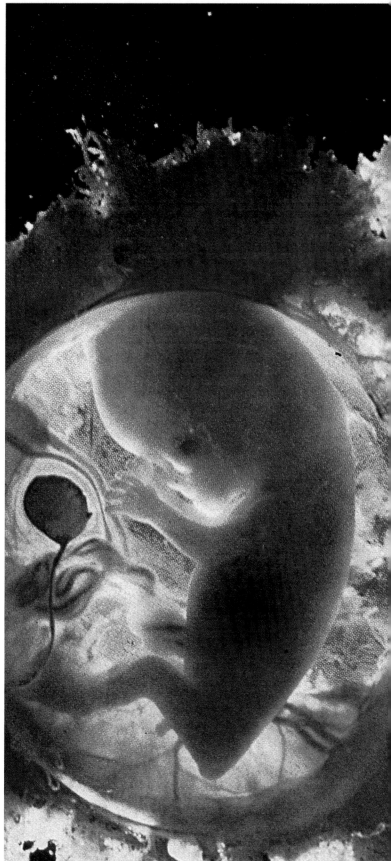

In the 1960s some women in Europe were given a drug to prevent morning sickness. This drug, thalidomide, unexpectedly prevented the natural abortion of deformed fetuses. Today many of these children lead quite normal lives (left). Ultrasound (above) is a technique employed to reveal the health and development of the fetus and can be used at as early a stage as eight weeks after conception. By this time the fetus is already developing the organs and features that distinguish it as human. A few weeks later its arms and legs have reached the proportions they will have at birth and the body size starts to increase beyond that of the head (right).

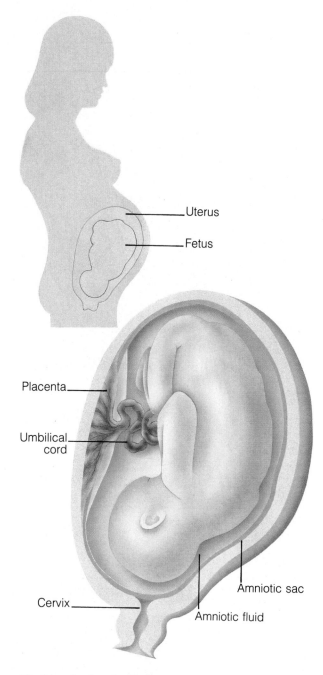

Uterus

Fetus

Placenta

Umbilical cord

Amniotic sac

Cervix

Amniotic fluid

The fetus develops inside the mother's uterus in a sac called the amnion, bathed in amniotic fluid. It is nourished by the placenta, an organ which develops only in pregnancy and which is attached to the uterus. Connecting the fetus to the placenta is the umbilical cord, which conducts nutrients and oxygen extracted from the mother's blood to the fetus, and carries away some of its wastes.

embryonic germ layers develop — the ectoderm, mesoderm and endoderm — which eventually become differentiated into all the various tissues and organs of the body. At this time, too, the notochord — the structure around which the vertebral column forms — materializes. The embryonic disk as a whole soon becomes pear-shaped, elongating with the growth of the notochord.

In these early days the fertilized egg and its associated tissues progress through stages which recall much more primitive life-forms. The mesoderm, for instance, from which the actual framework of the body is derived, becomes organized into regularly-spaced blocks (somites), giving the embryo a segmental appearance. By the end of the fourth week, it is beginning to resolve into a hunched creature — at one-sixth of an inch from crown to rump, barely larger than the height of this print — with a tiny, curved tail. The rudimentary heart (the first organ system to reach a functional state) is already beating.

The entire embryonic period, which lasts from the second to the eighth week, is one during which the organ systems of the body are being laid down. This is the period of utmost vulnerability to agents or substances in the environment which may cause damage to the unborn child. So far a number of such substances (most notoriously, the drug thalidomide) have been implicated in causing major congenital malformations which can be traced to disruption of development during the embryonic stage.

Rapid growth characterizes the whole period. From the fourth to the eighth week, the most critical phase of development, the embryo more than quadruples its length. If growth were to continue at this rate throughout the thirty-eight weeks of gestation human babies would weigh more than full-grown elephants at birth! Such a preoccupation with the size-for-date equation is by no means a frivolous one, for growth retardation is a potentially serious symptom in the unborn child. Crown-rump length is one of the main indicators of embryonic age. Males grow faster than females, and generally weigh more at birth.

Already at this stage ultrasound (sonography) can be a useful tool in determining the condition of the embryo. At least initially publicized as safe and

Ossification starts to occur in a fetus at about thirteen weeks after conception. A typical long bone first consists of plates of cartilage which grow and produce more cartilage, increasing the length of the bone (below left). *The cartilage along the bone shaft and at the heads then ossifies. It later erodes, the gaps being filled with cells called osteoblasts. Capillaries also fill the spaces, bringing blood to the* osteoblasts. *In this way the bone in the center of the shaft is replaced by fatty marrow. The extent of ossification is clearly visible by X rays in the sixteenth week of pregnancy* (below right).

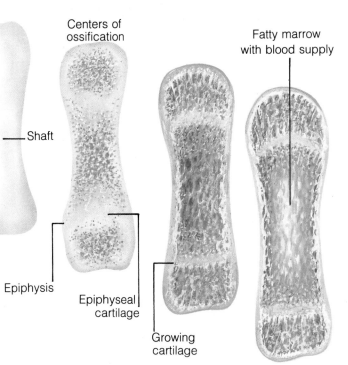

Centers of ossification

Fatty marrow with blood supply

Shaft

Epiphysis

Epiphyseal cartilage

Growing cartilage

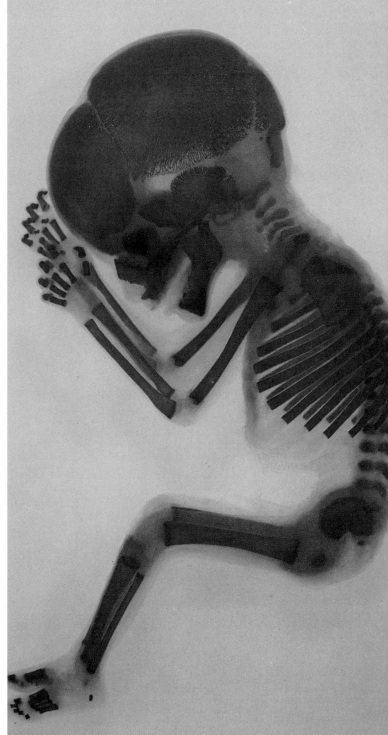

non-invasive, it can be used to delineate the contours and dimensions of embryos which are thought to be at risk, revealing any growth retardation or any one of a range of anomalies which might present a case either for some kind of intervention or, indeed, for termination.

Diagnostic ultrasound has also brought to specialist attention a curiosity unknown before the 1970s, when the technique came into use. This is the phenomenon of the vanishing twin. Twins are often seen on the viewing screen during the first three months of pregnancy but, at delivery, only a single baby is born. It is now believed that one of the two embryos may be lost — presumably reabsorbed in some way — in up to three-quarters of cases in which twins are conceived.

From Embryo to Fetus

By the eighth week, which marks the transition from embryo to fetus, the beginnings of all the main organ systems have been established. By now, although the "segments" are still present, the fetus is recognizably human — no more than an inch in length and with arms and legs, lips, nose, eyes and

even eyelids. The fetal period, which lasts from now until birth, is one of partial maturation of tissues and organs laid down during the embryonic period, and one of sheer growth. In the following month, the fetus doubles in size and assumes proportions closer to those familiar at birth.

The head constitutes almost half the fetus at the beginning of the ninth week, although the body then begins to catch up, doubling its length by the end of the twelfth week. In the final weeks of the first trimester (three months) of pregnancy, all four limbs grow rapidly, the arms in particular reaching their final relative proportions; the fetus begins to produce urine, which now becomes an important constituent of the amniotic fluid; the sex of the fetus becomes evident from the external genitalia (which can be detected by ultrasound); and the fetus begins to move, although this activity is not yet apparent to the mother. By the end of this trimester all the major systems of the body are developed, and the crown-rump length of the fetus is nearly three and one-half inches.

Sustaining all this growth is the developing placenta, the versatile, highly vascular, membranous organ through which the fetus obtains its nourishment and expels many of its wastes. Glucose is the main source of energy for growth in the womb. The insulin required for its metabolism is secreted by the fetal pancreas, which develops some endocrine capacity toward the end of the first trimester. Amino acids are also essential for fetal growth and metabolism, and these are also delivered by way of the placenta.

Growth continues to be very rapid during the first part of the second trimester (weeks thirteen to sixteen), by which time bone formation — ossification — is far enough advanced for the skeleton to be discerned clearly on X-ray film. From weeks seventeen to twenty, however, growth slows down. Brown fat (special tissue useful in heat regulation and production) begins to form at this time and the skin is covered with a cheese-like substance called vernix caseosa, a mixture of fatty secretion from the sebaceous glands and dead skin cells, as a protection against the effects on skin of long immersion in amniotic fluid. The body of the twenty-week fetus is covered in fine down, or lanugo (which may serve to hold the vernix to the

Quickening, the first fetal movements felt by the mother, usually occurs about the fifth month of pregnancy, when the presence of the child is obvious, as in Rembrandt's painting.

skin), and eyebrows and head hair are also apparent. During this period, too, the mother becomes aware of fetal movements.

Substantial weight gain occurs for the next month. This is significant from the standpoint of viability: it is most unlikely that a fetus weighing less than seventeen ounces, or whose gestational age is less than twenty-two weeks, will survive outside the womb, and so the period of viability is reckoned from this time — a cut-off point in some areas for therapeutic abortion. With expert post-natal care, fetuses weighing between seventeen and thirty-five ounces at birth may survive as what are termed "immature infants," but they, like those classed as premature infants (born at thirty-five to eighty-eight ounces), are at risk because of their immature physiology.

In the womb, of course, the possibility of reaching the full term improves with each passing week. There is further substantial weight gain between weeks twenty-one and twenty-five, although the body is still rather lean in appearance. Between weeks twenty-six and twenty-nine the lungs mature sufficiently to be able to breathe air, if necessitated by premature birth. The eyes, which are seen to close during the ninth gestational week, reopen during this period. The body begins to plump out. (During the last two and a half months, no less than half of the weight of the baby at birth is added.) The fetus usually rotates to an upside-down position at this time, so that the head can pass first down the birth canal.

Studies that use diagnostic aids to study the events that take place before birth have enabled researchers to eavesdrop on what one French embryologist engagingly calls *La vie clandestine*, noting a range of activities which may begin as early as the fifth gestational week. Ultrasound studies have, for example, revealed a whole repertory of fetal endeavors, beginning with generalized whole-body movements in the late embryonic period and progressing to more refined and specific movements as time goes by. Aside from gross maneuvers, "hiccup," respiratory movements and hand-to-face movements have all been seen in the first trimester of pregnancy; sucking, swallowing and "sighing" in the second. During this phase, too, the hands are seen to clasp each other, to grasp

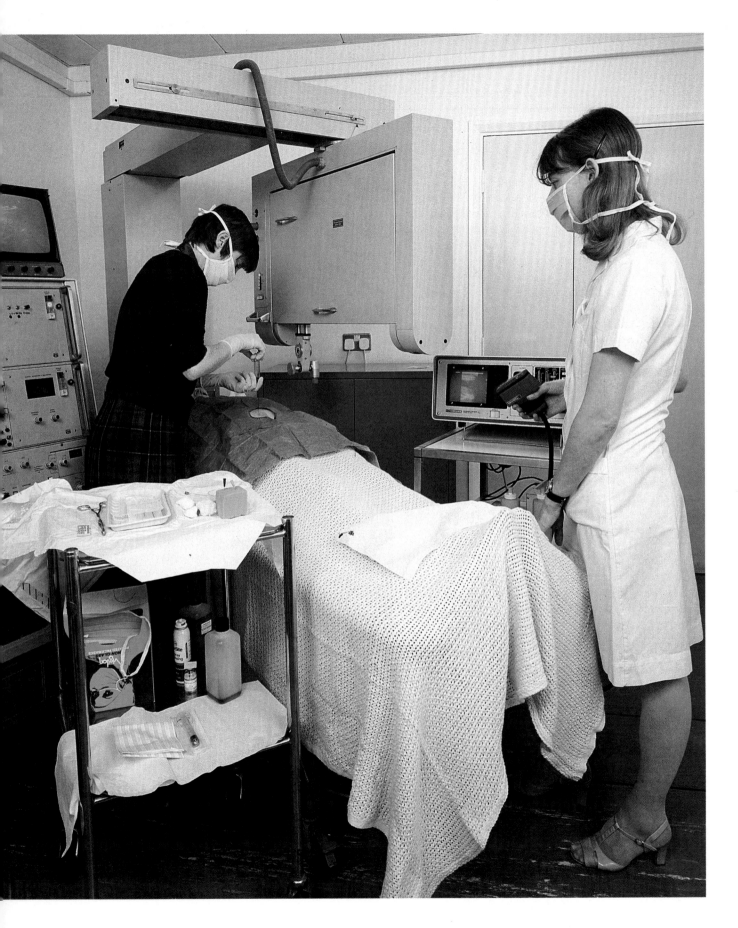

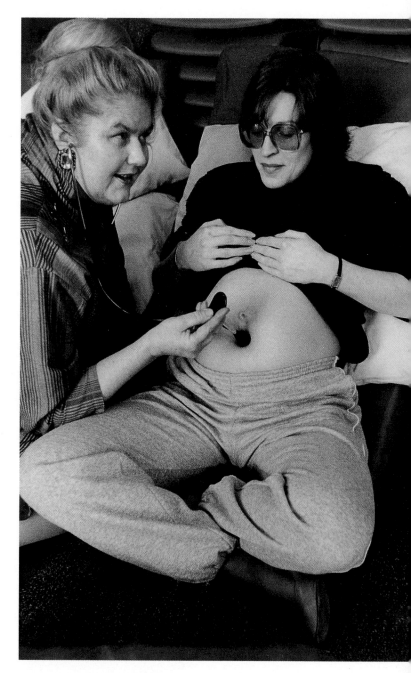

Amniocentesis (left) *involves drawing out a sample of amniotic fluid from a pregnant woman's womb. The fluid contains some of the fetus's cells, which can be analyzed to detect any abnormalities .*

the umbilical cord and to "explore" other parts of the body. This repertory expands and becomes more frequent with increasing fetal age.

From the second trimester onward, there are also responses to stimuli. If the hand of a ten-week-old fetus is tapped lightly with a thin object, it closes round the object. Later, stroking round the mouth may cause the lips to purse; nearer term, this same stimulus prompts the fetus to turn its head toward the source and attempt to suckle. Here is a small somebody, secure in a medium, who moves the arms and legs around, performs somersaults, sucks the thumb, yawns, sighs, passes urine, "inhales" amniotic fluid, goes to sleep, shields the eyes from light, and turns the head in response to sound.

Preparation for Birth

Now, as the time of birth approaches, there is a slowing of growth, although fat is laid down rapidly during the last six to eight weeks, rounding out the body contours. This finishing period is given over to a general building up of tissues and a steady progression to the state of systems-readiness required for the transition from life in the womb to an independent existence out of it.

At this stage concern may arise as to whether pregnancy can be maintained to term. Premature birth is still one of the most common causes of perinatal mortality (death in the time immediately before or after birth), accounting for no less than half of all deaths among the newborn. Premature babies — some seven percent of all those born in the United States — often have severe problems with breathing, circulation, nutrition and thermo-regulation. They are more vulnerable to infection, have weaker reflexes, and are likely to be jaundiced because of their immature enzyme systems. As one team of researchers has pointed out: "Neonatologists attempt to simulate an intrauterine environment as nearly as possible, but an artificial substitute for the placental supply-line has not yet been achieved." Most premature infants survive, but even with superlative care some may face difficulties later in life.

When the pregnancy goes to term, birth can be expected at the end of the thirty-eighth week, on or about day 266 after fertilization. At least as often, the calculation is made from the day of the onset of

The birth specialist Sheila Kitzinger listens to the sound of the heartbeat of a fetus which is thirty-five weeks old to make sure that there are no signs of distress or disturbance. Such prenatal checks can diagnose any problems, and ensure that prompt action can be taken to maintain the health of the mother and the baby.

21

Hans Spemann

Embryologist Extraordinary

Spemann's work on the embryos of newts and, later, frogs was not only highly original but represented also a valuable contribution to biological science in general, in its application to human anatomical, developmental and evolutionary studies. However, in order to carry it out, he devised new techniques of surgery that paved the way for the advance of microsurgery.

Hans Spemann was born in Stuttgart, West Germany, in June 1869. Son of a bookseller, he was educated at the local school, completed compulsory military service, and went on to study medicine at the University of Heidelberg. A short time later, he switched to zoology. After graduating in 1894, he went to study for his doctorate at Würzburg University, and four years later accepted the post of lecturer in zoology in the Zoological Institute there. In 1908 he left to become Professor of Zoology in Rostock. During World War I he was Director of the Kaiser Wilhelm Institute of Biology in Berlin, after which he was appointed to the Chair of Zoology at Freiburg.

Spemann's major achievement was to clarify the sequence of development in the very early stages of a newt embryo, and to discover that many of these stages were

critical to each other and to continued normal development. Using his new surgical instruments, he managed to remove the piece of external tissue (ectoderm) that in a newt embryo would normally become the lens of the eye. Then he replaced it with another piece of ectoderm taken from a quite different part of the embryo. The transplanted ectoderm then "correctly" turned into a lens.

This showed conclusively to Spemann that at least at this early stage, aspects of further development rely on the prior development of adjacent areas of tissue – more basic structures – and that somehow the "instructions" are only then given for the formation of the next stage of growth.

Other areas of ectoderm were then also transplanted – and similar results were obtained, depending each time on whether the transplanted piece was relocated next to a more basic structure. Such structures, because they seem to hold the key to the formation of other structures around them, Spemann called "organizers"; the process of influencing development in this way he called "induction."

All this tended to suggest that tissue from almost any source might grow correctly if transplanted at an appropriately early stage into an embryo. Spemann therefore tried transplanting frog tissue into newt embryos. Although the "instructions" were "received" and the organs duly formed, they were frog organs and not those of the host newt. Induction thus turned out to be possible, but only along lines specific to the originator of the tissue.

For his research – applauded by scientists the world over – Spemann received the Nobel Prize in the year of his retirement, 1935. His work was detailed in his book *Experiments Toward a Theory of Development*, published (in German) in 1936.

He remained connected with the zoological department of Freiburg University until his death in 1941.

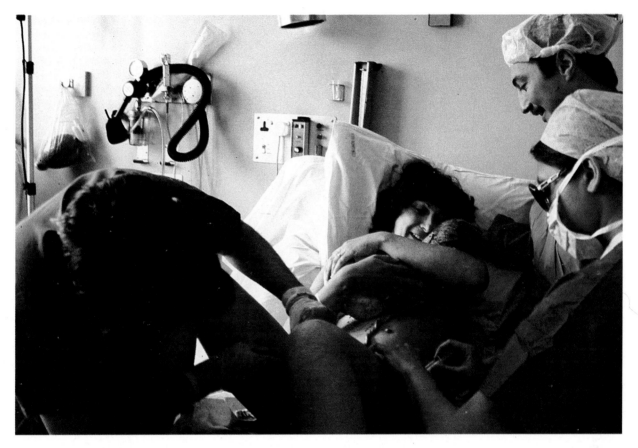

the last menstrual period, resulting in an anticipated birth date at the end of the fortieth week, on or about day 280. Most babies are born within ten to fifteen days of the due date, although some can linger in the womb for as much as an extra three weeks. "Late" babies are also at risk, because the placenta quickly degenerates after thirty-eight weeks and its capacity to provide nutrients and to exchange oxygen and carbon dioxide is reduced.

Timing of labor is less precise in human beings than it is in other mammals, and the reasons for this are not fully known. Maternal body chemicals, particularly hormones, have a significant role to play in birth (parturition). For instance, oxytocin — a hormone secreted by the posterior pituitary gland — acts as a uterine stimulant, and synthetic forms can be used to induce labor or intensify contractions; prostaglandins help prepare the cervix for dilation; and a group of compounds called catecholamines are also thought to be involved. In addition, the fetus itself makes some contribution, adjusting extracellular fluid levels and reducing urine flow, which in turn reduces the volume of amniotic fluid. But the specific trigger that sets labor underway remains unclear.

The Moment of Birth

Some authorities feel that birth in itself is a traumatic event for the baby — most notably, the French obstetrician Frédérick Leboyer, who through "birth without violence" advocates ways of minimizing the psychological shock of entering what he calls an "overwhelmingly confusing world." But the advocates of a more informal style of delivery remain diametrically opposed to practitioners of "state-of-the-art" hi-tech delivery in the setting of a busy metropolitan hospital.

A particularly controversial trend is the increasing recourse to Caesarean delivery. In the United States, the number of Caesareans has trebled since

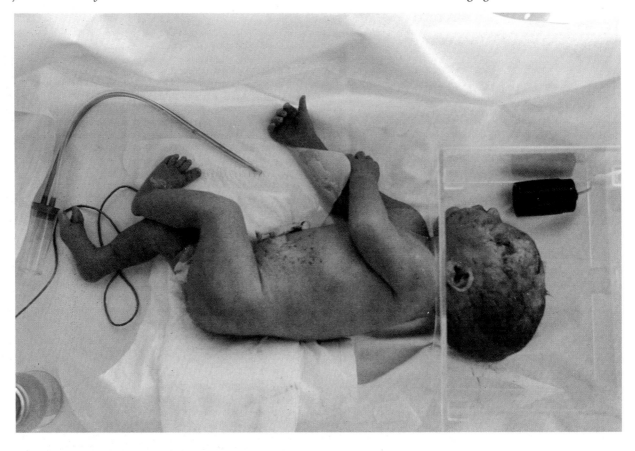

the 1960s and now accounts for up to twenty per cent of all births. Caesarean section does reduce the possibility of brain damage and may also prevent the transmission of genital herpes to the infant, but many obstetricians feel that Caesarean section should be performed only in an emergency — where there is immediate risk to the life of the mother or baby.

In the United States babies receive their first postnatal evaluation while still in the delivery room. "Apgar" assessments (named for Virginia Apgar, their originator) are made at one and five minutes postnatally of heart rate, respiration, muscle tone, reflex responses and skin color. Scoring is from one to ten (poor to perfect) by giving the mark zero, one or two on each of the five counts. Five times the maximum is thus a score of ten. Ninety per cent of neonates are graded at seven or above: they are a good color and have a lusty (but as yet dry-eyed) cry. Those scoring six or less need some assistance. Those with an Apgar score of less than four require treatment immediately. Every year in the United States some 200,000 babies receive intensive care.

An inability to breathe — asphyxia — is the first threat to the newborn, and may arise from a number of causes, from "cord problems" — constriction of the windpipe in some way by the umbilical cord — to some physiological deficiency in the neonate. At birth the lungs are soggy, half-filled with amniotic fluid. But already, from early in labor, the adrenal glands of the fetus have been releasing the hormone epinephrine, which speeds up the absorption of this fluid so that it can be replaced by air. As soon as the baby is born, the lungs should inflate. However, newborns have surprising resistance to oxygen shortage (there are many cases on record of infants being born alive up to twenty minutes after their mother's deaths) and, once respiration is established, the full-term infant

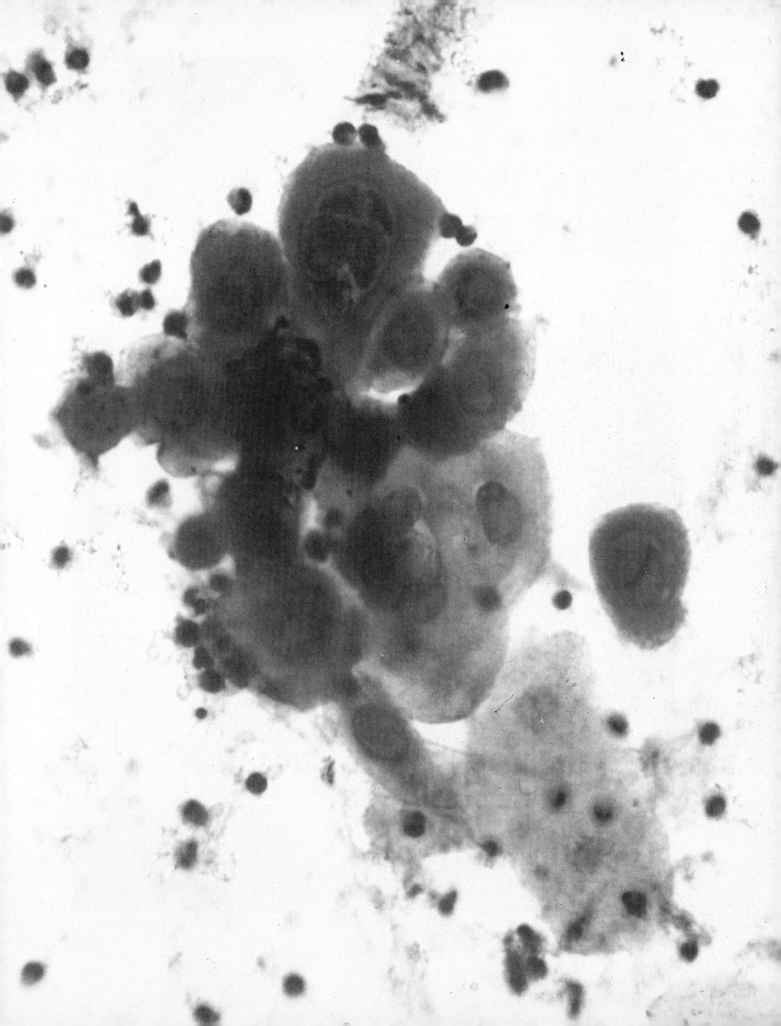

Pregnant women benefit from special exercises (left) *to strengthen muscles they do not normally use, and to aid relaxation. Medical precautions, even before pregnancy, are also advisable. For example, many*

physicians recommend that adolescent girls are vaccinated against rubella (below left), *because this disease, if contracted by a pregnant woman, can severely damage the fetus.*

Drug addicts who become pregnant are in danger of causing their unborn children to become addicts as well, which has happened in the case of this mother and child (below), *both of whom need treatment.*

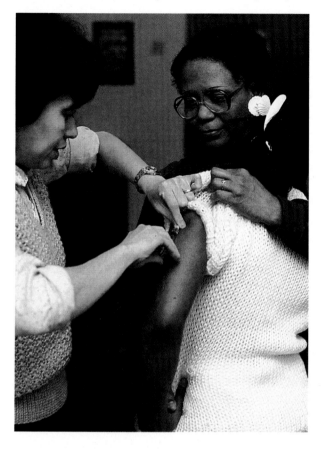

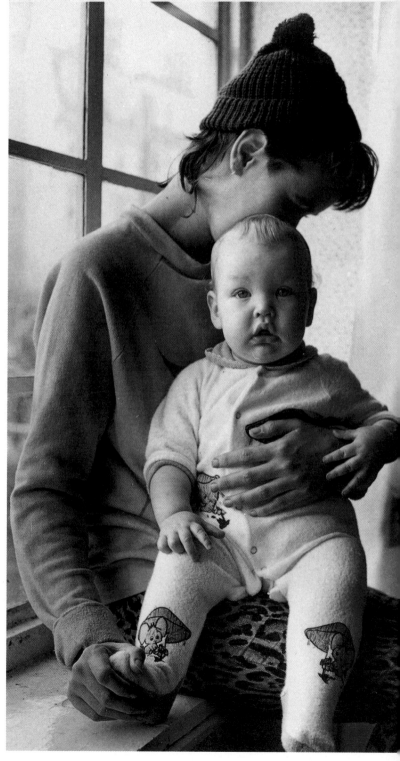

shows great powers of recovery. In the aftermath of the Mexico City earthquake in September 1985, for example, newborn babies were rescued alive after having been buried in rubble for nearly two weeks.

At birth, the average full-term baby weighs between six and nine pounds and is about twenty inches long. The head still accounts for about one-quarter of the total length. The forehead is high, the nose rather flat, and the face may appear chinless at this time. The skin is soft, dry and wrinkled; the whole body may turn a darker color when the baby cries. He or she almost always has blue eyes (the color may change later). Vision is a little blurred, and the hearing may be slightly impaired for the first day or two because of the presence of fluid in the auditory canals.

But already each newborn child knows the sound of the mother's voice and can respond to stimuli. Tiny, immensely vulnerable, each one has a range of reflexes — already rehearsed in the womb —

Having been fed for nine months on nutrients delivered through the placenta, it is a shock to the system of a newborn child to receive mother's milk. This first "proper" meal—the initial milky secretion, or colostrum—stimulates the gastrointestinal system, encouraging active digestion. The principal medical advantage of breast milk is that it contains antibodies which help build the child's immunity against disease.

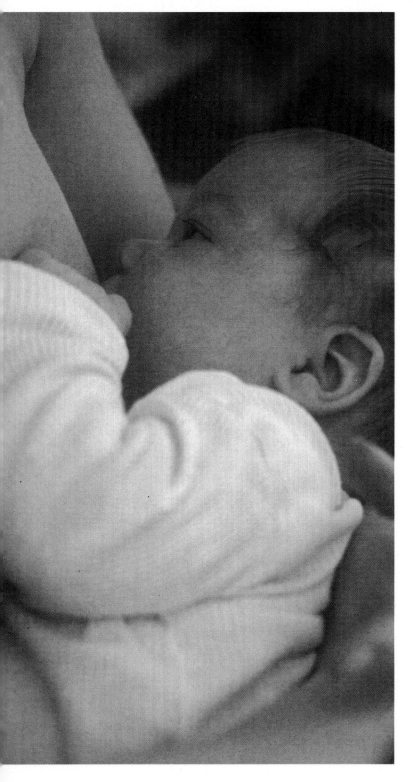

which immensely assist survival in the first few critical months of independent existence.

Matters of Life and Death

The first few days are most critical of all. It is now that the newborn, nurtured for so long in the buoyant medium of warm fluid, must adjust to a rather chilly, air-breathing world. And they must do so with patently immature systems. The primitive part of the brain, for instance, is mature enough to control life-support mechanisms, but the cerebral cortex is not fully functional and "brain-wave" or electroencephalograph (EEG) readings taken at this time may appear flat.

As the placental circulation shuts down, the circulatory system must become an independently functioning unit, and this involves the automatic, immediate and permanent closure of several suddenly obsolete pathways (those which had allowed the fetus to receive oxygen without the use of the lungs). The kidneys also are immature, although no great strain is to be placed on them yet because hormones preserve the balance of body fluids in the first few days of independent life, to maintain blood-pressure and prevent dehydration.

The baby now faces a vast number of adjustments. In the womb, the fetus receives only products carried in the mother's blood and derived from food which has been digested, absorbed into the mother's bloodstream and delivered to the fetus at a constant rate through the placenta. Now in a breast-fed baby the immature digestive system receives a shock dose of colostrum, the thin, yellowish fluid sometimes known as first milk. It is this first "meal" which causes a surge of hormones to stimulate gastrointestinal motility and paves the way for active digestion and absorption.

Meanwhile there remains the dilemma that, in the developed world, an infant is statistically more likely to die in the immediate perinatal period than at any time in the first fifteen years of life. In the United States, the infant mortality rate seems to have leveled out at just under eleven deaths per thousand live births (although for socioeconomic reasons, losses among non-white infants are almost twice as high). The American figures are better than they were in the mid-1960s, when the rate was 14.7 deaths per thousand.

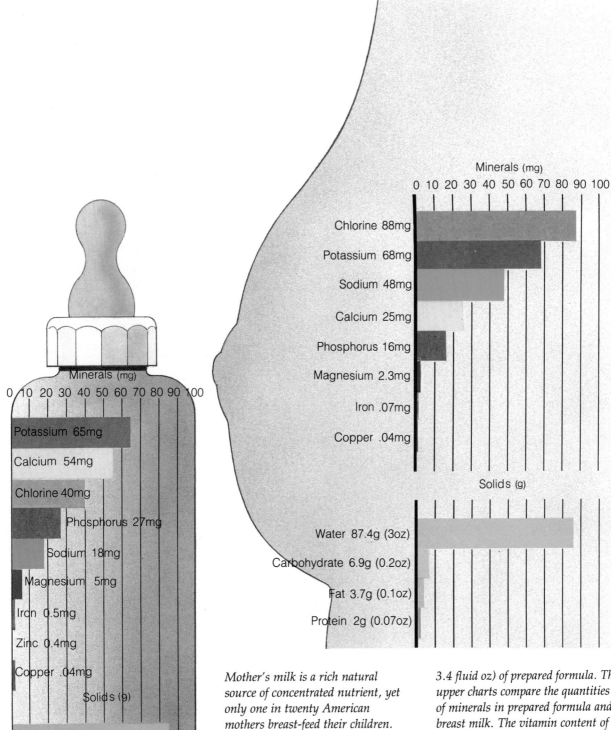

Minerals (mg)
0 10 20 30 40 50 60 70 80 90 100

Potassium 65mg
Calcium 54mg
Chlorine 40mg
Phosphorus 27mg
Sodium 18mg
Magnesium 5mg
Iron 0.5mg
Zinc 0.4mg
Copper .04mg

Solids (g)

Water 85g (3oz)
Carbohydrate 7.3g (0.25oz)
Fat 4.2g (0.15oz)
Protein 3g (0.1oz)

Minerals (mg)
0 10 20 30 40 50 60 70 80 90 100

Chlorine 88mg
Potassium 68mg
Sodium 48mg
Calcium 25mg
Phosphorus 16mg
Magnesium 2.3mg
Iron .07mg
Copper .04mg

Solids (g)

Water 87.4g (3oz)
Carbohydrate 6.9g (0.2oz)
Fat 3.7g (0.1oz)
Protein 2g (0.07oz)

Mother's milk is a rich natural source of concentrated nutrient, yet only one in twenty American mothers breast-feed their children. One of the reasons for this is that formulas for bottle-feeding have been produced which approximate the contents and quantities of nutrients in mother's milk. The contents of 100 grams (100g or 3.5oz) of mother's milk are very similar to those of 100 milliliters (100ml or 3.4 fluid oz) of prepared formula. The upper charts compare the quantities of minerals in prepared formula and breast milk. The vitamin content of each is approximately the same. The scales measure milligrams (mg) of mineral per 100g of fluid. The lower charts compare prepared formula and breast milk in terms of their content of carbohydrates, fats, proteins and water, expressed here in units of grams per 100g of fluid.

Chapter 2

Studying Growth

Today, the mechanisms of growth and development are studied by sophisticated means, and at the molecular level. Highly complex experiments on cells from a variety of plants and animals, not just those of humans, are used to delve into the secrets of how life is formed, develops and grows.

It is an obvious fact of life that children carry on growing until their teens or early twenties and that after this growth slows down, then stops. Two hundred years before the birth of Christ, this phenomenon of a limited period of growth was attributed to a concentration of blood within the small bodies of children. It was thought that as they grew, the blood's concentration decreased until equilibrium was achieved and growth stopped. By the eighteenth century, scholars had altered their views and explained that the farther the extremities grew away from the center of the body, the longer and narrower grew the vessels carrying fluids; thus the growth process slowed and eventually stopped. After more than twenty-one centuries of study scientists now believe that growth ceases when cells run out of "capacity." Non-experts could be forgiven for thinking that science is little nearer a satisfactory answer than were such early scientists as Aristotle.

Early Observations

Aristotle believed that the driving force behind growth and development was the sperm from the male. The sperm acted on the menstrual blood from the female and from it formed the several parts of the human body. For Aristotle growth and development took place in such a way that all the parts of the body took shape at the same rate. The driving force of development was, for him, a kind of psychic force — a spiritual agency that dictated the course of events. Unlike some of the people of his time he did not consider the parts of the body to be preformed in the sperm, just waiting to be enlarged during pregnancy.

Childhood is a time of great strides in growth and development, as well as one of excitement, adventure and discovery. Children's curiosity and eagerness to learn, as well as their almost boundless energy, are crucial ingredients in healthy development. Outdoor activities can help foster development and strengthening of the muscular system. Using the body is one of the keys to progress — if muscles are not exercised, for example, they simply waste away.

31

The tradition of tightly bandaging a baby, or swaddling, is an old one, and contrasts dramatically with current beliefs that young children should be allowed to grow with as few physical restrictions as possible. Here the infant Jesus Christ is depicted in "swaddling clothes," as are some of the tiny victims in the painting opposite.

Despite many intervening scientific advances, including the discovery of sperm and eggs as a result of microscopic studies in the seventeenth century, the working out of the stages in embryo development, which did not come until the nineteenth century, and the gradual understanding of the process of conception, it was not until the dawn of the "genetic age" of biology that any true advance was made in a proper understanding of the way in which growth and development are in fact controlled.

The gene, basis of control of all living things, was discovered as a direct result of the work of the Moravian monk, Gregor Mendel, and his experiments on peas and other plants. Only in the 1950s, which witnessed the elucidation of the structure of the gene's primary chemical deoxyribonucleic acid (DNA) by James Watson and Francis Crick at Cambridge University, England, did the driving force behind development finally and definitively begin to become clear.

In the three decades since Watson and Crick's discovery that changed the face of biological science, the gene and its actions have been studied with fervent intensity. Now it is known that the genes control and regulate all the processes of growth.

Milestones of Growth

As life takes shape, both within the womb and in the time following birth, growth proceeds hand in hand with development, the one dependent in some degree upon the other. But while development can be thought of as a continuum, lasting from conception to death, growth ceases after a certain time and consists of certain stages that are reasonably well defined.

The ancient scholars divided the milestones of life into sections of seven years, called the hebdomads. The mystical number seven originally came from the number of heavenly bodies visible to the naked eye — the sun, the moon and the five planets nearest to earth. It is thought that this preoccupation with the hebdomads accounts for the tradition that a girl reaches womanhood (experiences her first menstruation) at the age of fourteen when in fact, from an analysis of surveys carried out throughout more recent centuries and

among peoples of undeveloped countries, it seems the girls probably experienced the menarche a few years later.

As early as in the year 460 B.C., Hippocrates observed that environment affects the final height of an adult, and Aristotle gave a good indication of the maturing rate of children in 200 B.C. when he noted that at age five a child is about half adult height. At present this age is about two years, although the children of factory workers in the nineteenth century were not reaching the halfway mark until a year or two later.

During the Middle Ages and the Renaissance, very little was researched or written about the physiology of growth and hardly any new ideas emerged. But in 1571 a son was born to the personal physician to the King of Bohemia and Hungary. His name was Hippolyt Guarinoni and, after working in Milan as a page, he was schooled in Prague for eleven years. From there he went to study medicine

The natural desire to protect children is evident in the almost universal horror felt when children are harmed by adults. This is epitomized in the painting of the Biblical story of the massacre of the innocents, ordered by King Herod the Great in an attempt to kill the infant Jesus.

at the University of Padua at the time when the renowned Italian scientist Galileo was the Professor of Mathematics there.

Guarinoni became a physician in a town near Innsbruck (then in Germany) and, with an almost naive love of all things rural, he extolled the virtues of a country life and the dangers of the excesses of affluence. He can be regarded as the first voice of public health concern in Germany. He suggested that growth was retarded if a child was emotionally unhappy and noted that the menarche among the country girls was later than in the town. He reasoned that the rich food of the townsfolk produced fat girls, and indeed today early menstruation is common in overweight adolescents. Modern experts point out that Guarinoni's observations tally with those made today among adolescent girls in agricultural communities in undeveloped countries.

The Age of Enlightenment

At the end of the seventeenth century in Europe, there was to be a refreshing clash of ideologies between the Puritans and the apostles of the new Enlightenment about the nature of children. The rod-wielding Puritans viewed babes as bundles of sin to be "broken." ("Iniquity is co-natural to infants.") Progressive thinkers such as the English philosopher John Locke (1632–1704) believed that the child was born with his mind as a *tabula rasa*, a blank slate; his or her intellect and personality were molded by events. Mercifully, although most child-rearing propaganda prior to the eighteenth century was written by the Puritans, it was the new Enlightenment that caught on.

Support for this wholly new concept of the child as the product of the environment came from a quite unexpected source: the discovery of Tahiti. Captain James Cook (1728–1779) and his men reported that Tahitian methods of child-rearing were vastly different — and much freer — than those practiced in the West. Following such revelations it became fashionable for philosophers to theorize over "natural man."

As the new Enlightenment spread, the facts of child welfare remained depressing. As the eighteenth-century physician William Buchan pointed out: "Almost one half of the human species

The transition from a rural to an urban life style brought much hardship in the nineteenth century, especially to families that lost the father or breadwinner. In rural communities there was usually someone — a relation or a neighbor — to care for the children, whereas in the cities the widow and her offspring would have to survive as best they could, often by begging, as this painting The Pinch of Poverty shows. The rise of welfare and other forms of state support for poor families coincided with society's recognition of this fundamental change brought about largely by industrialization and urbanization.

perish in infancy by improper management or neglect." In Western Europe in the eighteenth century the plight of the poor, and especially the children, was indescribable. Chroniclers of cities at this time show that, around the affluent core, there were abysmal shanty-towns and slums peopled by ragged, half-starved wraiths. There were abandoned or vagrant children, and the mortality among these in particular was atrocious. Even among the affluent section of society, the rate of growth was lower than it is today and child mortality was high.

One of the most charming indications of the rate of maturing in Europe came from the records of the Bach choir in Leipzig. All the choristers were boys and information about their entry into boarding school included their father's professions and their date and place of birth. After careful analysis based on the number of bass, tenor, alto and soprano voices in each choir, experts have recently deter-

mined that the choristers' voices were breaking at around the age of seventeen, very much older than the present-day average of about thirteen. During the years of the War of Austrian Succession (1740–1748), the average rose by six months, probably because of the deprivation and starvation brought about by the war.

The first real growth studies were carried out by the military, particularly Frederick William I of Prussia (1688–1740). He was the father of Frederick the Great and wanted the guards of his palace to be the tallest men in the continent. With this aim he sent scouts out to scour Europe. One of the largest recruits brought in was a Norwegian who was six foot four inches tall, and exchanges similar to the exchange of spies across the Iron Curtain today were arranged with other countries. This collection of giants was the antithesis to a collection of dwarfs made earlier by Catherine de Medici (1519–1589) to entertain the courts. Unfortunately for her scheme,

all the marriages between the dwarfs were without offspring.

Other recruit studies show that soldiers were not only shorter in the past than they are now, but that they continued growing slowly for longer. From a Norwegian recruiting survey carried out from 1818 to 1823 emerged the fact that cottagers' sons were on average an inch and a half shorter than the sons of wealthy farmers, and that the extra length was in the legs. The first study of children was probably at the Carlschule in Stuttgart between 1772 and 1794, and from there emerged the same conclusion that richer children were taller. One of the first national surveys was in Sweden in 1748, made in an endeavor to find out how strong a fighting nation Sweden was as far as available military manpower was concerned.

The situation was similar in England. In fact after Thomas Coram's Foundling Hospital opened in London in 1741, it was reported that two-thirds of

Goblins and bogeymen, invented by nineteenth-century adults to frighten naughty children, surround the idyllic safety of the fairy nest, where only the best-behaved child could hope to go.

the 15,000 infants admitted over a five-year period died, allegedly due to "the profuse waste and imperfect workmanship of nature." Losses were the same at the Foundling Hospital in Paris, and in Dublin the infant survival rate went as low as ten per cent. Yet, somehow the burials began to tail off. Populations started to increase — slowly at first, but gaining momentum from the mid-eighteenth century onward.

The reasons for the demographic shift of the eighteenth century are complex. There were advances in public health awareness, accompanied by a gradual improvement in the level of parental care. For the first time, physicians began to address parents directly on the subject of their children's health. Michael Underwood's *Treatise on the Diseases of Children* (1789), for instance, was directed to "intelligent parents, as well as the medical world" (and was distributed in North America, Britain, France and Germany by the middle of the following century). William Moss, an obstetric surgeon with an eye on the potential market, saw to it that his *Essay on the Management of Children* (1781) was "purposely adapted for Female Comprehension, in a manner perfectly consistent with the Delicacy of the Sex."

But the real gains lay in a growing recognition of the need for public health measures, such as improved sanitation, moves to restrict contagion, and upgrading of institutional care of the sick. In a period of expansionism, it was England that led the initiative toward public health, and an Englishman who pioneered the breakthrough which, more than any other perhaps, signposted the way to the conquest of infectious disease: Edward Jenner introduced the practice of vaccination, initially against smallpox.

The Experts of the Nineteenth Century

Now that the problem of sheer survival was finally being brought under control, the climate was even more conducive to the reappraisal of children. Unlike the moralists of earlier centuries, to whom childhood in itself was of no intrinsic interest, at the dawn of the nineteenth century society in general began to take a keen interest in how children functioned — and how they might best be encouraged to develop. So building on the work of men such as John Locke and Jean Jacques Rousseau — whose *Émile* was probably the first widely-read child-rearing manual of its time — the theorists flocked to their publishers.

The primary approach was to direct the attention of parents to the needs of their own young, and much of the written output, of course, concerned the practicalities of child rearing. Baby care, for instance, became a field in its own right, and volume after volume was devoted to such matters as bathing, dressing and feeding. One of the earliest and best books by a woman was *Domestic Duties* (1825) by Mrs Parkes. "The cry of an infant should never be disregarded," admonished Mrs Parkes; "It is Nature's voice."

This great wave of concern was spreading throughout Europe. In Brussels Adolphe Quetelet (1796–1874) founded modern statistics; in France a physician named Villermé (1782–1863) began to study the poor and stated "easy circumstances prolong life, poverty shortens it"; and in Britain

Edwin Chadwick (1800–1890) collected data on the miserable lot of the working classes and factory children.

Quetelet was primarily an artist and secondarily a mathematician. His greater mentor was the poet and scientist Goethe. Quetelet was the first person to carry out a cross-sectional survey of a population of children, and between 1831 and 1832 he made one survey of height and one of height and weight. His aim was not so much as a spur to reform, but rather a search for the perfect ''average'' man in the artistic sense, the *homme moyen*, yet he did observe that development was altered by ''climate, differences in nutrition and greater or lesser amounts of labor.''

Villermé had more altruistic intentions. He was a surgical assistant during the Napoleonic wars and stayed with the army for ten years, witnessing the most appalling deprivations. His experiences were the basis of his thesis on the Spanish campaign in Estremadura, and after leaving the army he

To escape from religious intolerance, and to make a better life for their families and children, various groups of people emigrated from Europe to help colonize new lands. Although they were making a fresh start in an often hostile environment, the hard but healthy and active life style they established not only led to larger families, with less child mortality, but also seems to have resulted in an increase in stature, probably because of an improved diet. Typical of such immigrants were the Pilgrim Fathers, who included Separatists from Puritan England. They arrived in New England at Plymouth Bay at Christmas in 1620. This engraving, based on a painting by George Boughton, shows pilgrims walking to church through the snow.

A girl sews as her sisters watch or play in Alexis Harlamoff's painting The Young Seamstress. *During the last century it was believed that helping the development of girls' mental powers was a waste of time and that girls needed little formal education. Today views on such matters are considerably more enlightened, and the general policy in Westernized nations is one of equal opportunity for all.*

returned to medical practice. He analyzed the records of conscripts at a time when many in France felt that a long-term result of the Napoleonic wars had been a national decrease in the height of men. The tall men had fought and died abroad and the country was still reeling under the burdens of starvation. It is interesting that neither Villermé nor Quetelet considered inheritance as playing any part at all in the height of offspring.

In the notorious textile mills of northern England children of three or four were sent crawling beneath unguarded machinery to pick up cotton waste. Older children were forced to work up to fifteen hours a day. In many places children of eight or less spent up to twelve hours a day working in the inky blackness of coal mines. Children were also used in gangs of agricultural workers and had to travel long and arduous miles to and from work and toil from sunrise to sunset.

Edwin Chadwick was deeply involved in the research behind the various Acts passed in order to improve the working conditions of these children. His surveys were thorough and used good controls; information was gathered on deaths, stillbirths and accidents. The results spurred two reformers, Samuel Stanway and J. W. Cowell, to make further measurement surveys in the Manchester Sunday Schools which were attended by both factory children and nonworking children. The results were predictable. The factory children were very much smaller, in fact shorter than the smallest three per cent of today's population, and eventually most of them attained a height in adulthood of less than five feet.

The Factories Regulations Act was passed in 1833, setting an age limit of nine (below which children could not work) and reducing the numbers of hours, but Leonard Horner (1785–1864) felt that the 1833 Act did not go far enough. The report he prepared in 1840 on the conditions in the mines created such a furor that women and children were banned from mine work completely. Horner did not investigate the milestones of development, but James Whitehead, a surgeon from Manchester, estimated that factory girls in 1830 experienced the menarche at about age fifteen, two and a half years later than is usual today.

It is now known that the working conditions

In 1796 the British physician Edward Jenner discovered that the dreaded disease smallpox could be prevented by vaccination. This statue shows a child being vaccinated by Jenner.

were not the only culprit in this crime of stunted growth. Malnourishment of the pregnant mothers began a tendency that poor working conditions only worsened. Low birthweight babies suffered the same severe undernourishment as their mothers had done during pregnancy. It was common practice to quieten babies with opiates such as Godfrey's Cordial and Mrs Wilkinson's Soothing Syrup which, as a contemporary writer observed, "in many cases established a calm that was but a prelude to a deeper quiet."

Only one other set of records revealed a section of children in society who were even more growth retarded than the factory children, and these were the boy convicts transported from England to Australia from 1788. The reasons are easy to see. The children were usually convicted for stealing, most probably food, and they came from the most deprived backgrounds imaginable. On average they were almost three inches shorter than the

Fat and contented angel-children, or putti, *decorate the fringes of many works of art, such as this painting of the Virgin Mary by Peter Paul Rubens. This idealized representation in fact shows the children to be unhealthily overweight, from today's health-conscious point of view, although in Rubens' time it may have represented a desirable sign of prosperity.*

factory boys by the time they were eighteen. It is interesting to compare these statistics with those pertaining to other sections of society at the time. The tallest group was found at Edinburgh University where, in 1834, the average was the same as it is for present-day British men — about five foot nine inches.

Despite the Factories Act of 1833 conditions remained bad in the north of England and the death rate among babies was very high indeed. Pregnant women worked right up to the birth and had to return within the month to retain their posts. Unable to leave their machines for five or six hours at a time, mothers could not feed the babies at work and many were left with inadequate child-minders. In 1872 a group of doctors set out to collect data from many schools in the north of England. What emerged was that merely living in a factory town was not the cause of retarded growth. It was the work itself and all the social aspects of being a factory worker. The results of the survey cul-

minated in the Factory Act of 1874 and further improvements for these workers.

More affluent people were not totally free from the devastating death rate among children at this time. Diseases such as typhus, smallpox and scarlet fever preyed heavily on children everywhere. Today in Western societies it is expected that nearly every child born will survive, but parents of the nineteenth century often lost as many as half their children. Charles Darwin, for example, had ten children, three of whom died. It is said that Darwin nursed his ten-year-old daughter Annie during her final illness, and twenty-five years after her death he could not speak of her without tears welling in his eyes.

Growth Studies in North America

The study of human growth in North America really began with Henry Bowditch (1840–1911), when he presented a paper in 1872 at the Boston Society of Medical Studies. Bowditch was not only

the cofounder of the American Physiological Society but also the Dean of Harvard Medical School from 1883 to 1893. Surveys had been made before this, but not for the same reasons. A census had been carried out in 1624 in Virginia and after the Abolition of the Slave Trade Bill was passed in 1807 careful records were kept to prevent the smuggling of illegal slaves. Trading within the country was still allowed, the slaves being transported by coastal steamers. Every slave embarking or disembarking was recorded by height as well as age and sex. These figures have been analyzed recently and, to compare them with the factory boys of England, the average male slave was more than three inches taller than the English factory boys at the end of his growing period. A study of slaves in the Caribbean at the same time shows that they were not as tall as the slaves of America and neither were the children of the Irish immigrants in Boston.

But back to Henry Bowditch. The paper that he presented was based on measurements taken every year for twenty-five years of thirteen women and twelve men, all from one extended family, and the records were kept on the backs of the doors in their New England home. Henry is one of the named participants, and although no one knows for certain who the family was, it may have been Bowditch's own.

By plotting the graphs using the information available, Bowditch noted that at the age of about twelve the girls, persistently smaller than the boys, suddenly began to outgrow them. At fourteen and a half, the boys began to catch up and reset the boys-taller pattern. The girls had almost finished growing by this age, but the boys continued gradually to gain height until they were about nineteen. Between 1880 and 1910 Bowditch's Law of Growth referred to his definition of the adolescent growth spurt at puberty.

Bowditch instigated the collection of a great deal of statistical data through the Massachusetts State Board of Health, and he urged School Committees to set up surveys of schoolchildren similar to the one he had instigated in Boston.

In Milwaukee the schoolchildren were taller and heavier that those in Boston, and in St Louis, William Porter added another dimension to his

Breakfast under the trees, with the family dog joining in (left), may have amused the children of rich parents, but the sons of workers in industrial towns were more likely to be found working in factories.

SLAVE AUCTION

One of the many iniquities of slavery in the Southern States before its abolition in 1865 after the Civil War was the way it caused the breakup of families. Often the father was bought by a farmer to work on his plantation, while the mother and children were sold to someone else as domestic servants. This may have affected the children's physical development.

survey when he compared growth with ability at school. At this time children moved through grades at school when the work was complete, regardless of age, and Porter noted that the quick maturers made up the high grades. For example, a fifteen-year old in a low grade weighed less than a fifteen-year old in a high grade. (A similar trend had been noted in 1893 by a Russian researcher.) Porter's observations caused much controversy, particularly because he implied that the trend was irreversible. Franz Boas (1858–1942), another great man in the study of human growth, strongly disagreed and stated that ''a retarded child may develop and become quite bright.''

Auxology — The Study of Growth

Boas carried the study of growth through into the twentieth century, and with his methods of analyzing the data he gathered, he advanced the science of auxology. He reassessed the surveys of the Boston children made by Bowditch, and showed that not only did different social and ethnic circumstances alter eventual height, but also that they altered the rate or tempo at which a child grew.

During the adolescent growth spurt, height and weight increase peaks at a particular age, and this age occurs younger among well-nourished healthy children.

Boas produced the first national standards for height and weight in North American children in 1898, after collecting further data from nearly 90,000 children of school age. The results showed that American-born children were taller than their counterparts anywhere in Europe, although they were smaller than children of the same age in the United States today.

But it was Boas' study of immigrants and their children, which he published in 1912, that really rocked the boat of accepted anthropology. Until that time there had been an unshakable belief that the size of a person's head, expressed scientifically as the cephalic index, was constant within a race, and this law had been used to trace the origin of many tribes and peoples. Boas showed that children born to immigrants and growing up in America were not only taller, but that their heads were larger. The cephalic index was not inherited — it could be changed by a better environment. As the British expert on child health and growth,

J. M. Tanner, wrote in 1981: "When Boas showed that even the central tabernacle of the doctrine — the cephalic index — was built on sand, they chorused their disbelief and displeasure."

Collecting Birthweights

Most of the surveys described so far dealt with children of school age. But during the same years a group of physicians and obstetricians were collecting data on newborn infants, in an endeavor to improve the appalling death rate within the first year of life. One of the first things that is done today at a birth is to measure and weigh the baby, but this was not common practice in the eighteenth century.

In Dublin, however, where Joseph Clarke (1758–1834) was Master of the Lying-In Hospital, moves were made to find reasons for the death of half the children born there. The mortality rate was greatest immediately following birth and more boys than girls were dying. Clarke set out to prove that his theories were correct — that boy babies were larger and that not only did the larger head size account for difficult deliveries, but the bigger baby died sooner from inadequate nourishment.

In Paris similar measurements were taken, and by the time James Simpson (1811–1870) was making similar records in Edinburgh, the general pattern was clear — boy babies were bigger than girls. But the vulnerability of the boys could not be completely explained by size alone, as was proved by Gustav Viet in 1855 when he took the figures from a Berlin clinic and showed that among boys and girls of the same weight the death rate was still higher among boys. Viet was also the first person to note that second- and third-born babies tended to be smaller than firstborns, and in 1864 Matthew Duncan in England showed that the baby's birthweight generally increased with the age of the mother.

In 1892 Pierre-Constant Dubin (1846–1907) set up the first well-baby clinic in Paris, and data on the growth of babies began to flood in. Dubin called his clinic *Goutte de Lait* because it supplied milk to needy mothers and children. Similar centers started up throughout France, and by the beginning of the twentieth century England had followed suit. All children attending the clinics were weighed, and from this information the biochemist T. Brailsford Robertson (1884–1930),

For centuries children have been employed as beggars, or have been forced to adopt this way of life to survive. The beggars' "targets" in the old painting of Venice (above) were probably tourists, who are still prime candidates for this role in many African and Asian countries today. In countries where begging is no longer necessary for survival, some still persists in the form of collecting for good causes. Asking "trick or treat" or singing Christmas carols for charity (far left) are all enjoyed by children as well as by the donors, who usually regard it as a pleasure to give.

who was professor at the University of California and later at Adelaide, Australia, set out to compare English children with their Australian counterparts. He discovered that although the birthweights were similar, the English babies did not thrive as well and by six months they were stuck in the lowest tenth centile from which they never broke free. As far as England was concerned, much still needed to be done.

Modern Welfare Movement

In 1920 a Child Welfare Movement began in the United States devoted to studying the "whole child," and many of the most influential Americans in the field of human growth were involved. Their influence on the educationalists and reformers was and continues to be very strong.

In 1930 a White House Conference was set up under President Hoover to protect children during the depression years. It is interesting to note that among the many growth studies made during the 1940s, data was amassed in a way that would be impossible today. X rays were taken at the Harvard School of Public Health of many bones in normal children's bodies, a practice abandoned now because of the dangers of leukemia from low levels of radiation. In the 1930s and 1940s the doses used were probably far above those now regarded as "safe."

Auxology has benefited many nations in many different ways. Originally it highlighted groups of society at risk and gave powerful ammunition to reformers. Today, armed with data from the many surveys that are still being added to, physicians can look at a child and decide whether he or she is one of the range of normal children in the nation, or whether some underlying disorder or emotional stunting lurks. We must not become complacent. In a report to the President from the White House Conference on Children in 1971 it was aptly stated

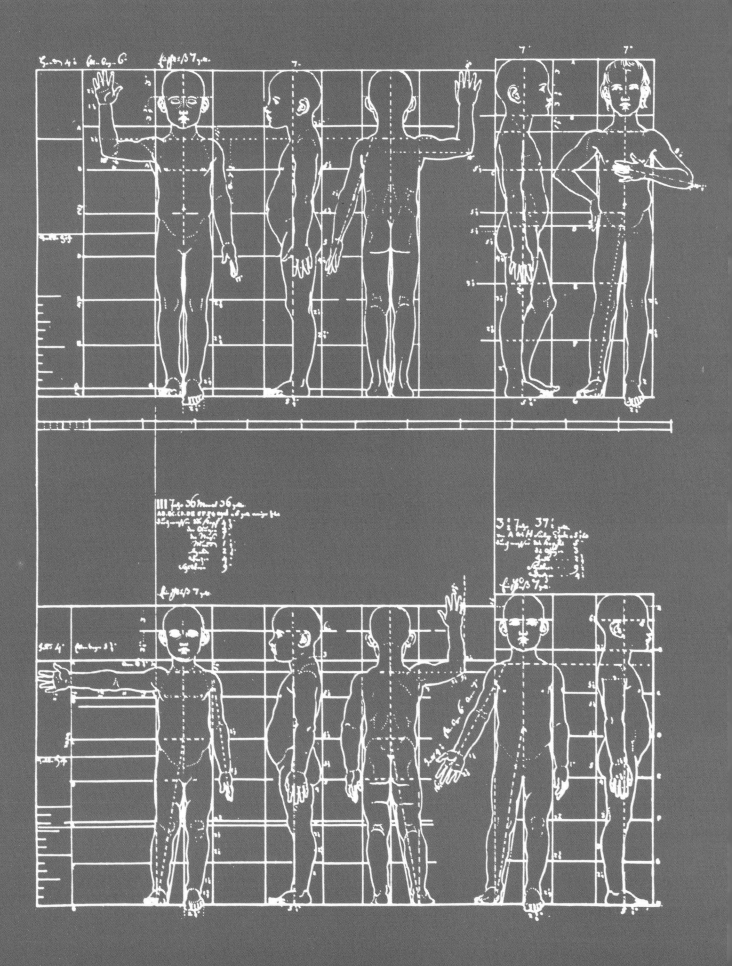

PRENATAL GROWTH

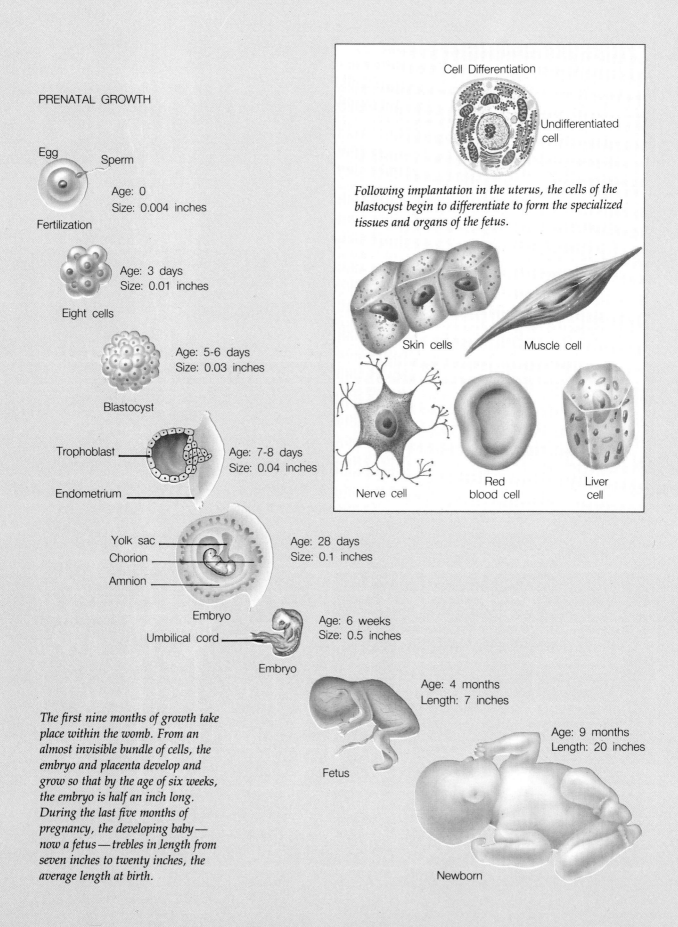

Egg
Sperm
Age: 0
Size: 0.004 inches
Fertilization

Age: 3 days
Size: 0.01 inches
Eight cells

Age: 5-6 days
Size: 0.03 inches
Blastocyst

Trophoblast
Age: 7-8 days
Size: 0.04 inches
Endometrium

Yolk sac
Chorion
Amnion
Age: 28 days
Size: 0.1 inches

Embryo
Umbilical cord
Age: 6 weeks
Size: 0.5 inches
Embryo

Cell Differentiation
Undifferentiated cell

Following implantation in the uterus, the cells of the blastocyst begin to differentiate to form the specialized tissues and organs of the fetus.

Skin cells
Muscle cell
Nerve cell
Red blood cell
Liver cell

Age: 4 months
Length: 7 inches
Fetus

Age: 9 months
Length: 20 inches
Newborn

The first nine months of growth take place within the womb. From an almost invisible bundle of cells, the embryo and placenta develop and grow so that by the age of six weeks, the embryo is half an inch long. During the last five months of pregnancy, the developing baby — now a fetus — trebles in length from seven inches to twenty inches, the average length at birth.

6 months

The way in which a child's long bones grow is well illustrated by the bones of the hand. At birth, the only hard bones are in the fingers. Then, by the age of six months, two areas of cartilage in the palm begin to ossify. Bone formation in the palm continues, together with elongation

18 months

3 years

5 years

7 years

The rate at which children gain height varies with age and with sex. Most undergo two growth spurts, in early childhood and during adolescence, when many girls are taller than boys of their own age because their maximum growth rates generally occur two years earlier. Most girls stop gaining height by the age of about sixteen, whereas boys usually continue to grow until they are eighteen years old.

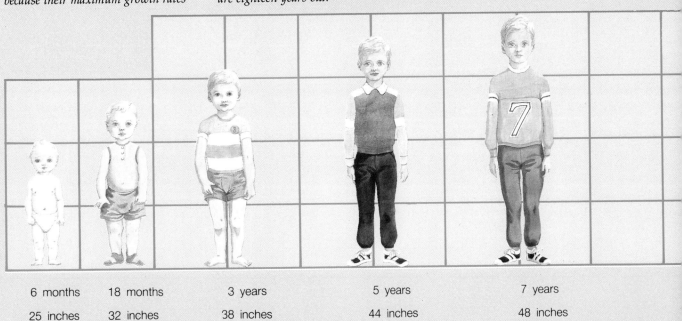

6 months	18 months	3 years	5 years	7 years
25 inches	32 inches	38 inches	44 inches	48 inches

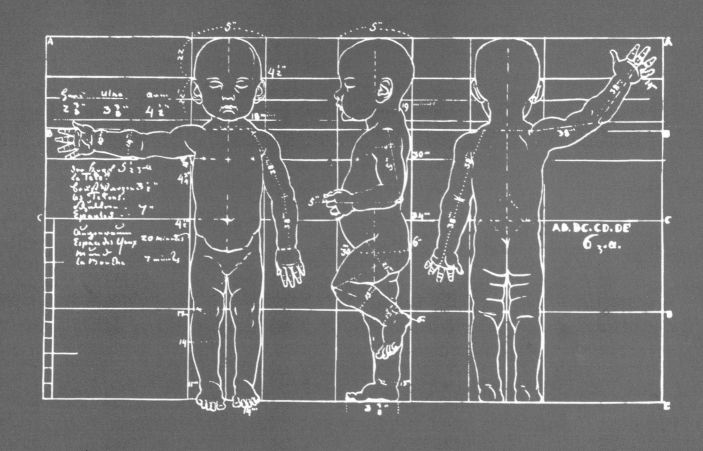

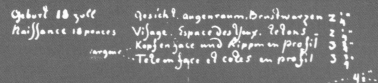

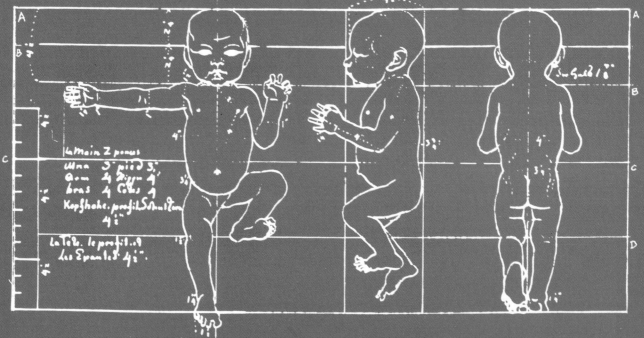

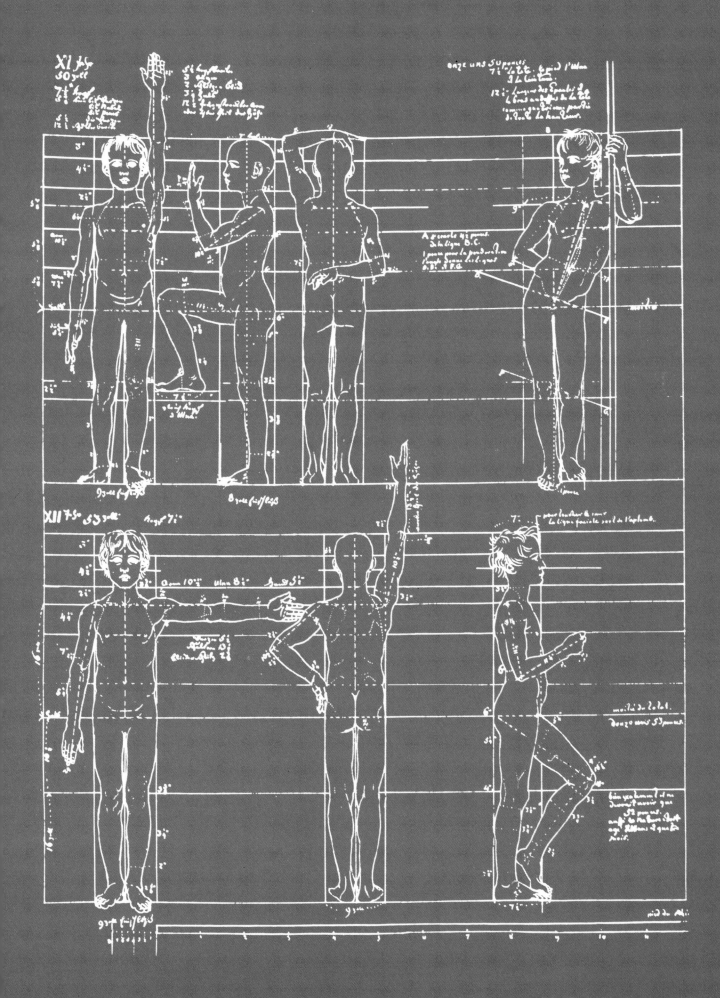

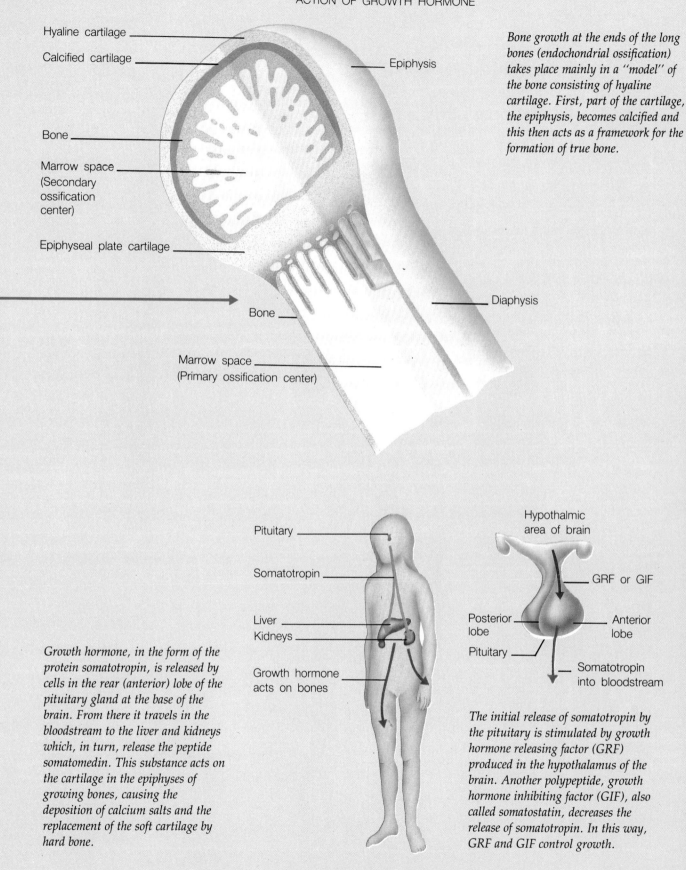

Hyaline cartilage

Calcified cartilage

Epiphysis

Bone

Marrow space
(Secondary
ossification
center)

Epiphyseal plate cartilage

Bone

Diaphysis

Marrow space
(Primary ossification center)

Bone growth at the ends of the long bones (endochondrial ossification) takes place mainly in a "model" of the bone consisting of hyaline cartilage. First, part of the cartilage, the epiphysis, becomes calcified and this then acts as a framework for the formation of true bone.

Pituitary

Somatotropin

Liver
Kidneys

Growth hormone
acts on bones

Hypothalmic
area of brain

GRF or GIF

Posterior
lobe

Anterior
lobe

Pituitary

Somatotropin
into bloodstream

Growth hormone, in the form of the protein somatotropin, is released by cells in the rear (anterior) lobe of the pituitary gland at the base of the brain. From there it travels in the bloodstream to the liver and kidneys which, in turn, release the peptide somatomedin. This substance acts on the cartilage in the epiphyses of growing bones, causing the deposition of calcium salts and the replacement of the soft cartilage by hard bone.

The initial release of somatotropin by the pituitary is stimulated by growth hormone releasing factor (GRF) produced in the hypothalamus of the brain. Another polypeptide, growth hormone inhibiting factor (GIF), also called somatostatin, decreases the release of somatotropin. In this way, GRF and GIF control growth.

of the finger bones at the epiphyses, regions of cartilage at their ends (shown in blue). Girls mature earlier than boys. The ages given are for boys; for the equivalent development in girls, subtract six to twelve months in childhood and up to two years from the teenage years.

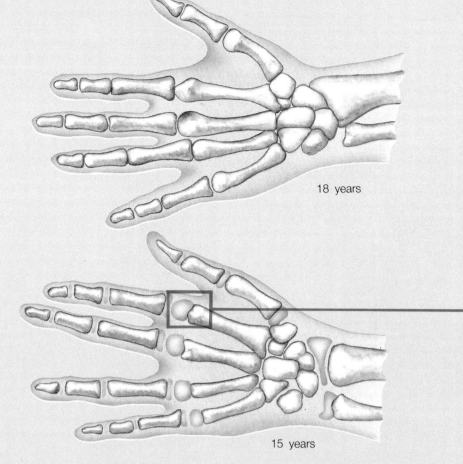

18 years

15 years

12 years

12 years

57 inches

15 years

66 inches

18 years

70 inches

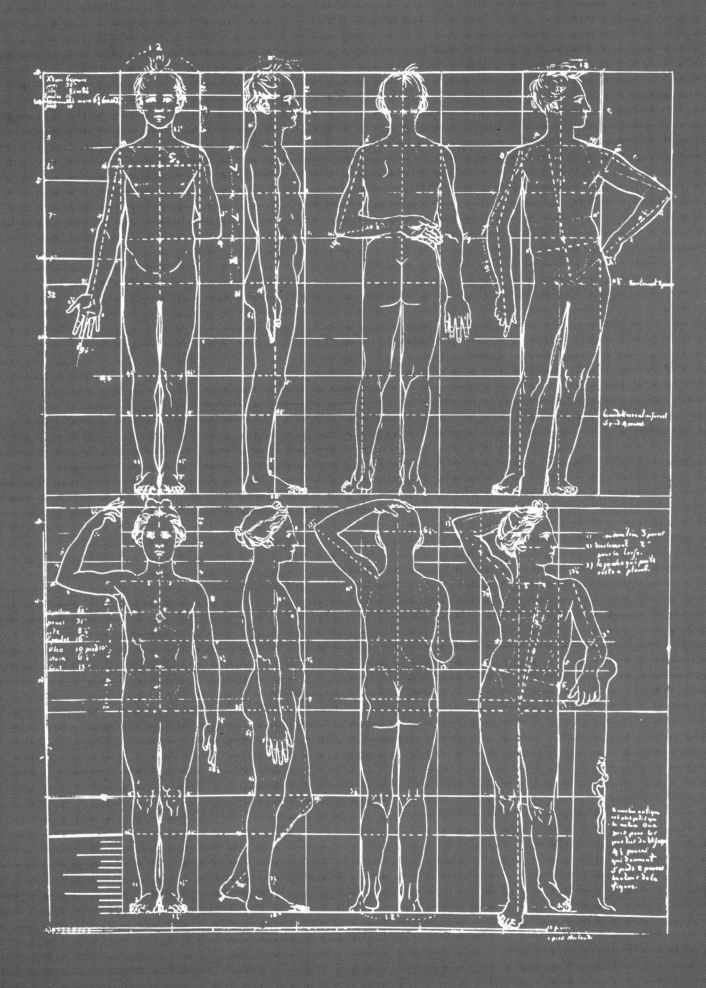

that "for families who can get along, the rats are gone, but the rat-race remains."

Modern Child Psychology

Throughout this time, other researchers began to study the development of children's minds. The statisticians were joined by the Austrian psychologist Sigmund Freud (1856–1939), who bestrode the later decades like a colossus. Brushing aside his detractors, Freud was able to demonstrate fairly forcefully the importance of the infant years in shaping personality; neurotic behavior in the adult, he maintained, often stemmed from events in childhood. Besides taking Europe by storm, his theories swept North America. It was G. Stanley Hall, founder of the American Psychological Association and arguably the first true developmental psychologist, who introduced Freud to the United States, inviting him to give a series of lectures at Clark University in Worcester, Massachusetts, in 1908.

The early years of the twentieth century were dominated by the IQ measurers, developmental psychologists and behaviorists. In 1905 a Frenchman, Alfred Binet, developed tests designed to screen out subnormal from normal children. (These were the precursors of modern IQ tests.) In the

D'Arcy Thompson

Growth and Form

Described by one commentator as "the first completely modern anatomist, in that his conception of [anatomical] structure was of molecular as well as of merely visible dimensions," D'Arcy Wentworth Thompson was author of a large and influential book, *On Growth and Form*, published in 1917. Also a mathematician distinguished enough to have had a mathematical paper published by the Royal Society, he was additionally a classicist of such celebrity as at one stage to be president of the Classical Associations of England and Wales and of Scotland.

Thompson was born in May 1860 in Edinburgh, Scotland, the son of a scholarly schoolmaster-author. Educated partly at home, he then went to the University of Edinburgh in 1878, and from there to Trinity College, Cambridge (England), in 1880. He was already a keen naturalist, and it was at the Cambridge Natural Science Club that he first read one of his papers (on the structure of joints and ligaments). Within two years he was being commissioned to edit and translate books on natural history.

He was then offered a teaching post at Cambridge, which he accepted. Apart from immersing himself even further

in his biological studies, Thompson also spent some of his time in social welfare work. A year later, however, he left Cambridge to take up the post of Professor of Biology at Dundee University, a position he then retained for more than sixty years. At Dundee he initially lectured on biology, anatomy, zoology, botany and embryology with a panache that became his trademark.

In academic holidays he traveled widely, throughout the world, often sponsored by government organizations either as a naturalist or as a diplomatic observer of fisheries or other maritime occupations. And so it was that in 1898 a senior post in the Fisheries Board for Scotland was made open to him; he took it, and kept that too for forty-one years.

It was in 1889, nearing his thirtieth birthday, that Thompson found his interest in mathematics truly awakened. Needless to say, it was in connection with the mathematical curves displayed in the structure of various marine organisms.

On Growth and Form was an extremely informative book that incorporated much of Thompson's vast knowledge. It set out to be both anatomical and evolutionary: to demonstrate *why* things grow the way they do, at least as much as *how*. Thompson's gift for mathematics meant that he had a ready grasp of the physical relationships between mass, movement and resistance, and in his adaptation of those principles to biological themes he was thus able to expound (for example) on the engineering technicalities inherent in the formation of the long bones in the human body, with clarity and authority. Some of his ideas on evolution are now seen as partly incorrect—but his exposition of statistical and structural detail remains extraordinarily well presented.

He died in June 1948.

1920s, doctor-psychologist Arnold Gesell began to compare age-related differences among children in physical, intellectual and social development; the Berkeley studies monitored children's growth, and Louis Terman and his colleagues at Stanford University began their famous studies of "gifted" children (some of their original subjects, now in their seventies, are alive and well and still being tested). An outcome of these researches were the Stanford-Binet intelligence tests.

In Europe after World War I, the brilliant Swiss biologist Jean Piaget — who was to become perhaps the most influential figure in developmental psychology — began probing the cognitive stages of childhood. He showed how children came to adapt to their environment. In the United States at more or less the same time, John Watson, founder of behaviorism, began to publish his work on child psychology and child-rearing practices. Watson's approach, although not exactly warm by late twentieth-century standards, was manifestly to train the child how to become an adult. These and other initiatives, however, were cut short — and their findings temporarily eclipsed for several years — by the realities of a second more terrible war.

Following World War II, and the subsequent "baby boom," parents were more than ever determined to do the right thing by their children and give them the almost proverbial "better start." But in the face of the mass of heavy scientific work on child care which had emerged prior to the war, where were they to begin? This dilemma was to a large extent resolved in general by the timely intervention of Dr Benjamin Spock. His message, a reassuring one in the 1950s, was simple: parents should relax and enjoy their children and quit worrying about whether or not they were doing them psychological harm.

Throughout the long history of the study of growth it has become increasingly clear that the development of mental, emotional and intellectual capacities, like physical growth, is determined partly by heredity and partly by environmental influences: what is provided by nature has also to be nurtured for the best results. As the study continues from now on, it is perhaps intriguing to consider that if as much progress is made during the next century as was made in the last, not only will much more be known but humans themselves may be capable of more development.

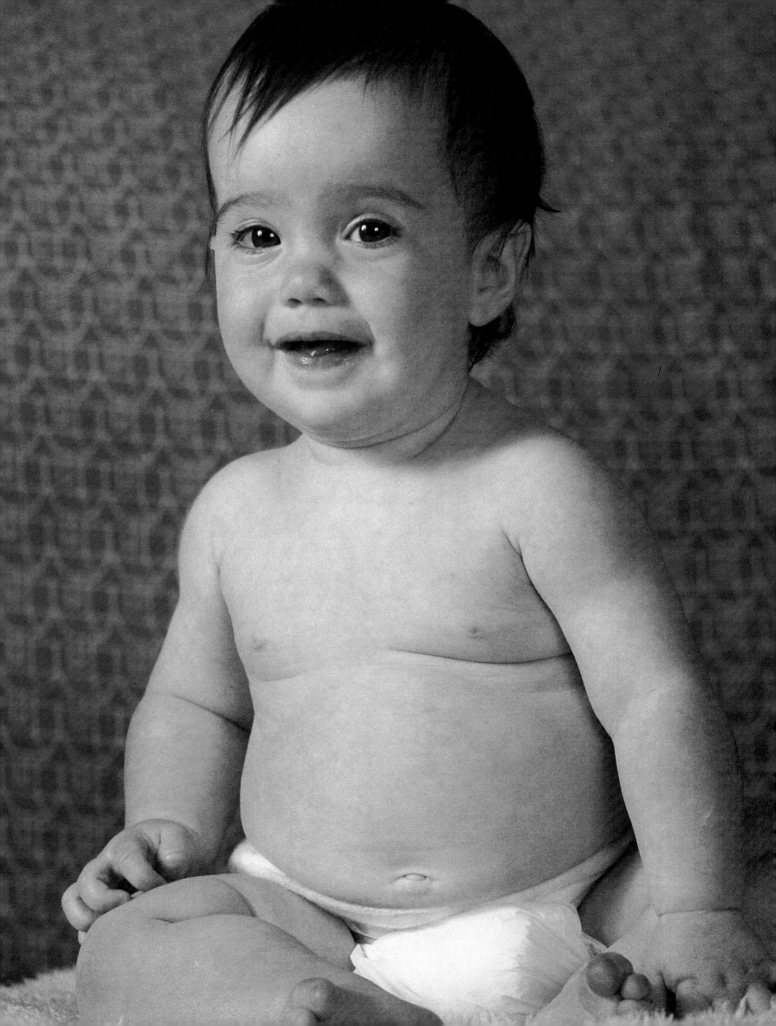

Chapter 3

First Encounters

Scientists have now definitively established by experiment something that mothers have intuitively known for centuries: babies need to be regularly picked up and cuddled to maintain their physical and emotional well-being. In other words, babies cannot grow and develop on their own, even if supplied with an adequate supply of food. The ingredient of care is vital to physical progress as well as to mental advancement.

In experiments, baby monkeys isolated from physical contact with their mothers during the first few weeks of life failed to thrive, not just emotionally but also physically.

Loving from Birth

At first a newborn baby seems completely helpless, but in fact there is an inbuilt survival system of reflexes and behavior. When a baby — say she's a girl — needs attention, she makes sure she gets it by crying. Her influence is strengthened by the emotional effect her crying has on her mother — she cannot be ignored; and within a few weeks her crying alone will induce the release of milk if her mother is nursing. Any mother finds it very difficult to leave a baby to cry, and if food is not what the baby needs the mother cuddles and talks to the baby to comfort her and the baby responds. Mother and baby are emotionally tied by a bond which ensures that the baby receives all she needs to keep her alive and sustain her growth and development.

To accompany this the baby has reflexes, some of which are essential for survival now, and some of which seem to have been part of survival techniques in the earlier days of the human race, when survival was a much less sure business than it is today.

A baby's sucking reflexes are very strong just before and after birth. The baby may even have suck marks on the hands or arms from sucking while still inside the womb. When a baby's cheek is touched, he or she turns the head toward the

Many years of adventure and discovery face the human baby commencing on the long road to maturity. Human beings are comparatively immature at birth and require a long period of development before they are capable of all the activities and skills characteristic of their species.

Everywhere this Nigerian mother goes, baby goes too. Close physical proximity in babyhood creates a secure and loving bond between mother and baby, forming the basis for interpersonal relationships in later years. An important factor in this bonding is believed to be the fact that a child held so close can easily detect the rhythm of the mother's heartbeat, just as he or she did when still in the mother's womb.

stimulus and the lips pucker. And when the lips touch the mother's breast, the nipple of a feeding bottle, or even a finger, the baby begins to suck. A premature baby however, may show a weak sucking reflex.

If a finger or pen is placed into the palm of the newborn baby, her hand closes tightly over it. This is the grasp reflex, and it is so strong that the baby can support her entire body weight for a few seconds. The reflex disappears during the third month of life.

The startle reflex is a series of movements the baby makes if her position is changed suddenly. She also makes the same movements in response to a sudden loud noise, or even to the trauma of having her diaper changed. Her head is thrown back and her arms and legs stretch out; she takes a sharp breath, and usually she cries. Perhaps once this reflex made her easier to catch if she lost her grip on her mother, but now it is a good indication that she is being handled too briskly.

A physician tests these reflexes when the baby is a few days old and has had time to recover from the trauma of birth and settle into some sort of feeding schedule. The reflexes give a good indication of the baby's performance compared with what is known to be normal. Many are initially absent in a premature baby. Most disappear by the time the baby is three or four months old, when her own voluntary actions develop and take over.

When a baby is four months old, a different defense reflex comes into play. If she is held with her head pointing down toward a surface, the baby adopts a "parachute reflex" posture, extending her arms above her head and opening her fingers as if to protect her head from the possibility of injury.

A physician may additionally test other reflexes, among them the "doll's eye" response — which describes the way the eyes do not follow immediately when a baby's head is turned slowly. Other tests include pupil reaction, which is tested using a bright light shone into the eye, as it is tested in adults; and the neck righting reflex, in which, when the head is turned to one side, the shoulders follow the head automatically.

Constant attention and feeding may seem an impossible task to a tired and emotionally labile mother shortly after birth, but many mothers find

Crying (below) *is the only way a newborn baby has to communicate. Most mothers learn to distinguish cries of hunger, tiredness, discomfort or those indicating that baby wants comforting* (right).

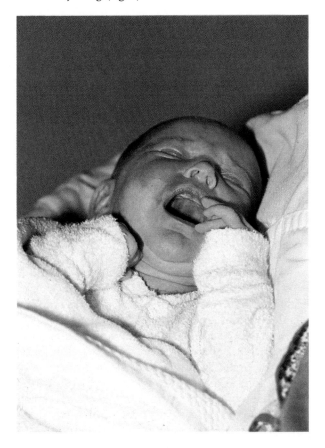

that by adopting a system that revolves around "demand feeding" — that is, offering breast or bottle whenever the baby needs it — they hasten the time when the baby settles down to a manageable eating and sleeping routine.

One of the first things to be checked when a baby is born is the overall weight; this is the starting point for measuring growth and development outside the womb. Many factors influence a baby's weight in such a way that it is not actually the average of just over seven pounds; boys tend to be a little heavier, for example, and a first baby tends to be a little lighter than subsequent brothers and sisters.

Heredity is also important — small parents tend to have small babies, large parents larger than average babies. This trend continues through to the final height of the young adult and is, like other human characteristics, genetically controlled. Height is a trait determined by the action of many

Cocooned in a safe, watery world the developing fetus (below) rapidly gains length and weight. After birth, weight gain—a measure of progress —can be checked by regular visits to the baby clinic (bottom).

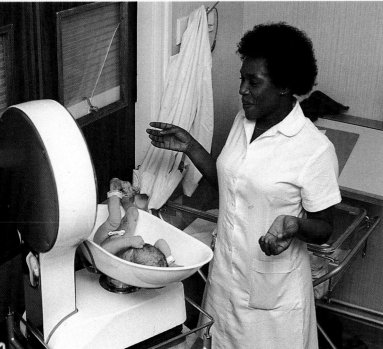

genes working together in unison to direct the rate and extent of growth from conception onward. These groups of genes, or polygenes as they are called, tend to be passed down the generations in blocks. This helps to explain why tallness or shortness runs in families.

The environment inside the mother can certainly affect the baby's birthweight. If she has been ill or is a heavy smoker, the baby may be smaller than expected — nicotine inhibits the uptake of oxygen by the fetus and oxygen is an essential requirement for cell growth. If the mother suffers from diabetes the baby may be larger than average because the cells have been supplied with an extra supply of the growth-promoting substance glucose. But despite these observations, birthweight and health are not mutually exclusive. A baby's health depends on the maturity and functioning of its systems, not on its absolute weight, be that ten pounds or five.

The aspect of weight that is important following birth is that babies should put it on after birth following a steady upward mathematical curve of weight gain and that they do not suddenly waver from that consistent pattern in any way which could indicate under- or overfeeding or some more serious latent condition.

In any case, for the first few days of life, many babies lose weight. This is perfectly normal, and the baby usually regains the birthweight in ten days. Large babies tend to lose more weight than small ones, but once birthweight has been regained, the baby puts on about five or six ounces a week. Again this is only an average amount — some babies gain faster, others gain slower, but all can be perfectly healthy. Most babies grow intermittently, so the more often the baby is weighed the more concerned the parents may become — unnecessarily — about the apparent speed or lack of it with which weight is put on. Weighing a baby every few weeks probably gives a better indication of development than does daily measurement.

Gaining Control of the Body

A baby has been born — let us suppose this time it is a boy. He lies on his stomach, buttocks in the air, knees bent underneath. He can just raise his heavy head off father's shoulder when held against

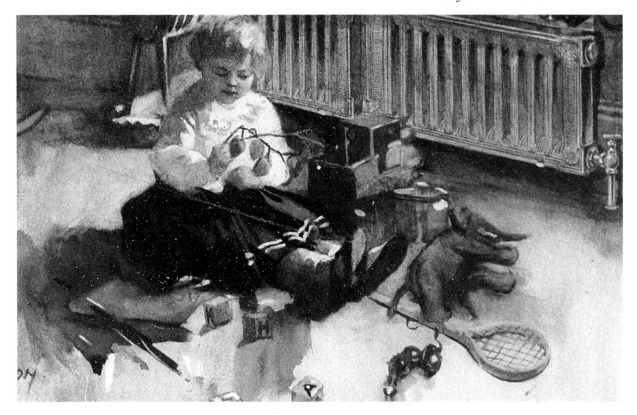

him, but most of the time he does not control his movements. When a newborn baby is lifted up by the arms the head would flop backward if unsupported. If held in a sitting position on a parent's lap the baby's back is comma-shaped and the chin sits on the chest. But by the age of six weeks a baby has some degree of control of the head, and as the weeks pass it gradually becomes less heavy in relation to the body and the muscles continue to strengthen. By seven to eight weeks the baby is strong enough to keep the body in line with the head when lifted from a lying position, and by four months braces the shoulders when lifted. By six months he can lift his own head off the bed when lying on his back.

From birth onward the baby gradually uncurls from the birth position. When he is lying on his front he bobs his head up until increasing strength allows him to hold his weight on his forearms — the pose of many early baby pictures. Both the head and the shoulders are off the mattress.

As time passes a baby has more control over position, and by ten weeks can roll from a side position onto the back — and less than four weeks after that can roll from the back onto the side. By six months he can roll over from his front onto his back and soon complete the turn the other way. The baby is on the move.

Once the baby has mastered neck and head control he is ready to go onto the next stage: learning to sit. At three months the back still sags, but by four months the sag is only at hip level and the head is secure unless the body is swayed. By six months he pulls up on adult's hands to try to get into a sitting position, and, once there, is strong enough to hold it. His only problem is one of balance; he needs support around the hips to keep him upright in the corner of an armchair, for example.

Throughout this process the baby is continually widening his or her mental horizons. By the time the baby can sit propped, he or she has become a real part of the family, entertained by watching people, and getting feedback from brothers and

Another milestone in development is reached as a baby discovers how to roll over. Motor development usually follows a regular sequence, with rolling over occurring at about six months of age.

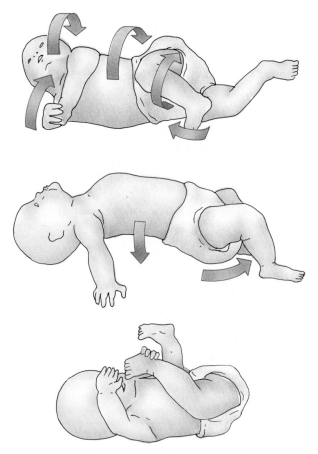

sisters as well as parents as they stop to play or chat. The baby responds with the whole body, kicking with pleasure and waving.

At first a baby balances by leaning forward and putting a hand on the floor to create a stable tripod, but by the age of one year can twist and turn around confidently to reach a toy. The baby may even shuffle along on the buttocks. Arm movements are becoming more refined, and a hand used like a scoop can pick up a toy.

Mobility Increases

It is important to remember that the "normal" ages for each type of behavior include a wide "normal" range — what some babies achieve at ten months may occur at twelve months or more in other babies. For example, it is very unusual for a baby to crawl before the age of six months, yet a baby may cover quite a distance while lying on his tummy by bending the legs underneath, pushing with the feet, then raising the front of the body on his arms — usually the direction of travel is backward. Care must be taken, however, not to leave the baby where danger looms — unattended on a bed, for example, or at the top of a stairway.

By ten months many babies have perfected a commando-style mode of travel in which they pull themselves along on their elbows and push with their feet while their stomachs remain on the floor. By eleven months, though, most babies can crawl with the stomach off the ground, and once that skill is mastered the baby becomes very adept at speedy travel — so much that he may wear holes at the knees and toes of his playsuit.

Throughout this time the baby has been preparing for the eventual skill of walking.

Soon the baby has control of the knees and feet and can stand, although he is still not good at balancing. At about eleven months most babies walk along holding onto the side of their crib, but the skill involved in sitting down again is not yet developed. Some babies stand and cry until an adult comes and helps, but others simply let go and sit down onto the mattress.

On Two Feet

Outside the crib a baby of this age uses furniture to pull up on, but often cries to be rescued because letting go means a fall. The moment he has been helped back to a sitting position he repeats the whole performance. Fortunately for all, this irritating phase is short-lived and if the baby is carefully helped back to a sitting position he will soon gain the confidence to try for himself. As with every new skill, a baby must practice again and again until everything is perfect before making the final launch. Balancing is a very complicated process, and however annoying a particular phase of behavior may seem to the parent, repetition is vitally important to the baby.

The next stage is a lurching movement. The baby still holds onto a support, but has gained enough confidence to shift his weight a little and take a shuffle to one side. As confidence increases even more, he puts hand over hand along the support and shuffles along taking more weight on a single leg at a time.

The age at which a baby leaves off lurching to take

A baby attempts to copy the actions of older children (below). Balancing actions such as these help to strengthen the muscles, which shortens the transition between crawling (bottom) and walking.

the first real steps varies enormously. It is preceded by a great increase in range — crossing small gaps, getting around the room from one piece of furniture to another. Eventually he meets a gap larger than the span of his arms and lurches across without sitting down. One day he lets go and stands, swaying slightly but finally balancing on two legs.

The giant leap to walking may still be a few weeks away. Sometimes a baby takes a couple of tottering steps then reverts to crawling for another month — realizing that it is quicker — before getting onto his feet again and walking with apparent ease. Other events may cause setbacks — an illness, or an emotional upheaval such as the arrival of a new baby in the home can make a baby give up lurching in preference to crawling, or abandon walking in preference to lurching. He will need to go through the learning stages again but the next time it will take a few days rather than weeks.

Apart from the nine months before birth, changes occur more rapidly during the first two years of life than at any other period. The attainment of physical skills such as sitting, crawling and walking depends on the maturation of the muscles and the nervous system. Although development is orderly, some infants reach each stage ahead of others. The left- and right-hand ends of each color bar give the ages at which 25 per cent and 90 per cent of infants, respectively, have attained a particular stage of development. The position of each baby gives the age when 50 per cent have accomplished that behavior.

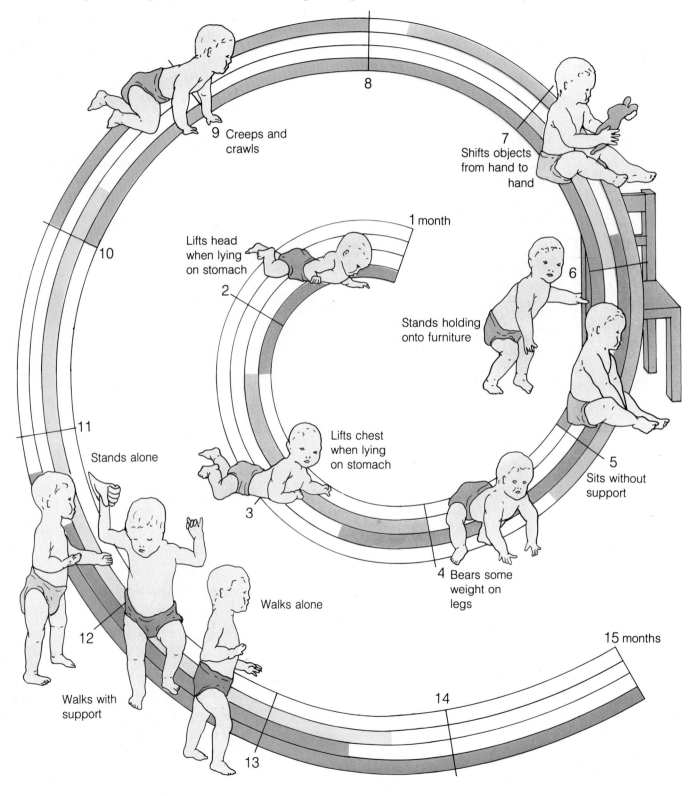

8

9 Creeps and
crawls

7
Shifts objects
from hand to
hand

10

1 month

Lifts head
when lying
on stomach

2

6

Stands holding
onto furniture

11

Stands alone

Lifts chest
when lying
on stomach

3

5
Sits without
support

12

4 Bears some
weight on
legs

Walks alone

15 months

Walks with
support

14

13

60

*Learning to walk is a baby's greatest
achievement. Encouragement is
needed to boost a baby's confidence
about standing upright, maintaining
balance and coordinating movements
for the first steps.*

The great advances in physical and mental skills of the baby in the year between birth and his first birthday are able to come about because of the way in which the brain and nervous system gradually mature over that period. When a baby is born, many of the nerves are not coated with the insulating, fatty myelin sheath that characterizes mature nerves. A nerve without such a myelin sheath is unable to take part in the complex relay system between nerve and muscle vital to coordinated voluntary action. By the end of the first year myelination of the nerves is virtually complete — a milestone that coincides in most children with the significant advance of being able to stand and walk unaided.

The brain, too, undergoes enormous development in both the first and second years of life. At birth, the average baby has a brain weighing only 26 per cent of what it will weight at adulthood. By the age of one the figure is around 55 per cent. On his second birthday a child will have a brain weighing only one or two per cent less than it will when he is twenty. The body is, incidentally,

remarkably well equipped to handle this enormous growth. There remain gaps and unclosed joins between the bones of the skull until about the age of four, which allow for the massive expansion in brain size in the first years of life.

By the age of fifteen months babies may be well into toddling, even if they still have to use crawling to get over to a support and up into a walking position. It is not until they are about eighteen months old that they are able to rise upright from a sitting position. Toddling is still fairly uncontrolled — babies are not good at stopping or at changing direction — and they have frequent tumbles. But a baby's bones are less vulnerable to injury than an adult's, and they do not have as far to fall, so most of the time the tumbles are not unduly upsetting for the child.

Progress from here on is extremely fast. By their second birthday toddlers are confident enough to walk, to stop and bend down to look at something, to point as they walk, and even to look backward over their shoulders. They are probably able also to play running games, to swerve and accelerate, and

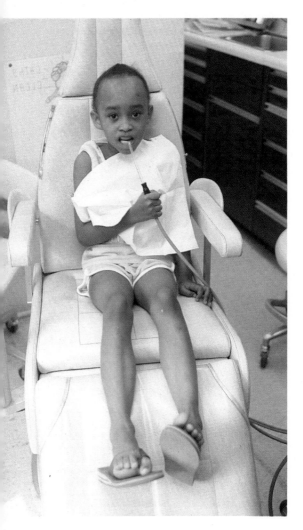

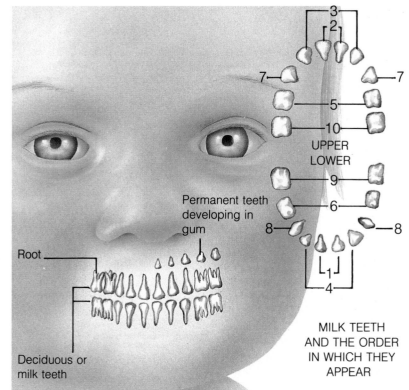

3

2

7 — — 7

5

10

UPPER
LOWER

9

Permanent teeth
developing in
gum

6

Root

8 — — 8

1

4

Deciduous or
milk teeth

MILK TEETH
AND THE ORDER
IN WHICH THEY
APPEAR

Teething (above right) can begin when a baby is about six months old. The lower middle incisors are first to appear, followed by the rest of the milk teeth during the next two years. Adequate care of the milk teeth is important because it establishes the dental health of the growing child and later that of the adult. For this reason most dentists recommend the use of fluoride, usually in the form of toothpaste, which helps strengthen the teeth. Further protection is often given by coating the teeth with fluoride after the appearance of the permanent teeth in later childhood (above).

possibly to kick a ball without losing their balance and falling over.

These achievements are commonplace but nonetheless amazing, particularly in consideration that no one has yet produced an efficient mobile machine that can coordinate such a complex system of joints and levers. (Most robots run on wheels, after all.) In addition, the bones of a child's skeleton are not only strong enough to take weight and tension as the muscles work on them, but are able simultaneously to grow.

The Development of Teeth

At birth a baby has milk teeth already formed beneath the gums. Occasionally, a baby is born with one lower incisor visible, but this is unusual. Babies tend to "cut" teeth during the second half of their first year, the front teeth (incisors) erupting first, followed by the upper incisors. There is little or no discomfort, but a baby's gums may be sore when cutting a large molar at the back.

Teething is a natural part of development and

does not cause conditions such as diarrhea, vomiting, fever or bronchitis. But some authorities state that the changing flora (the beneficial bacteria of the digestive apparatus) may cause diaper rash. Many mothers have observed that when a clean, well-kept baby develops diaper rash it commonly coincides with cutting a tooth.

It is important to care for the primary teeth as carefully as for the secondary, because loss of primary teeth not only causes pain but also alters the balance of the child's jaw before the secondary teeth are ready to emerge. A baby should be given water in preference to sweetened drinks, and sugary snacks should be kept for the end of mealtimes when the mouth is washed with saliva. Ideally, the baby's teeth should be cleaned after every meal or snack, but if this is not always practical, parents should at least be certain that a thorough clean is carried out last thing at night. Some domestic water supplies and many commercial toothpastes contain fluoride, a mineral salt that strengthens the protective coating of teeth, but

parents may ask advice from a dentist if there is reason to think the water in their area is low in concentration of fluoride.

A baby, bottlefed or nursed, who seems hungry only an hour after a full feed of milk, may need extra calories in the concentrated form of solid food. These can be introduced gradually from about the age of four or five months, when a baby is less likely to be fussy about changes in texture and has a less developed sense of taste, although some experts believe that weaning at too early an age is related to the development of allergies. It is traditional to start a baby off on cereals and strained fruit-and-vegetables, but a baby can be given most foods except the obviously highly-spiced types, and within a couple of months can certainly eat the family food mashed up to a manageable texture.

At this age a baby also enjoys food eaten with the fingers — toast, a cooked smooth bone with a little meat on it, or a slice of carrot or apple — but should never be left unsupervised when feeding himself. A baby soon becomes interested in

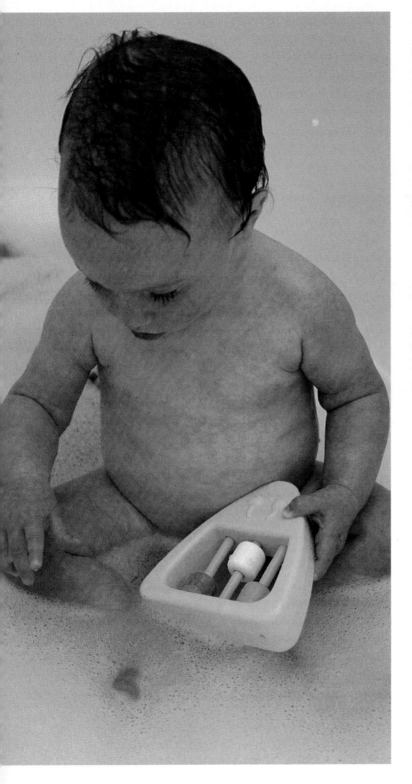

experimenting with food, squeezing it through the fingers and patting it. It is best to let a baby explore as far as possible: the handling of food may seem messy to an adult but to a baby it is just another of the thousands of new experiences.

Developing Senses

It is difficult to say exactly how much a baby can sense at birth or even before. Tests can show only that babies are distressed by some stimuli and apparently calmed by others. A congenitally malformed baby with no brain (anencephaly) shows a similar reaction to such stimuli, suggesting that much of the response is at the level of reflexes and may be the vestiges of nonessential primitive survival techniques. Bitter or sour substances in the mouth make a baby screw up the face; bottles of water sweetened to varying strengths, however, are accepted gratefully — and the sweetest substance is the one that is sucked the longest.

A newborn baby reacts unfavorably to a sharp sudden sound, but not to an equally loud but continuous noise (like that of a vacuum cleaner). Recordings of a mother's heartbeat soothe newborns and there is some evidence that babies are aware of more external sounds, such as music, when they are in the womb. Some researchers now believe that a fetus not only hears but retains memories of these experiences. It appears that adults retain basic responses that reflect a baby's stage of sense development, although these do not come to the fore until an adult has contact with a baby. For example, adults automatically pitch their speaking voices higher when "talking" to tiny babies. A baby responds to high-frequency noises but has little perception at the opposite end of the audible range.

At first a baby has little or no coordination between the listening sense and the seeing sense, but an observant parent knows that a baby is calmed by the sound of an adult voice alone, even if he listens without turning his head. A young baby is so sensitive to changes in tone that he may become distressed overhearing another child receiving a reprimand from a parent.

Initially the communication seems all one way, but usually within a week or so a parent can differentiate between cries denoting fear, pain or hunger. A few weeks later the baby adds to the repertory of noises with gurgles for pleasure and whimpers leading up to crying.

Human babies can see from birth — but they are very short-sighted. The part of the brain responsible for vision appears to need several, significant, months after birth to complete its development. Focus is fixed at about nine inches, almost exactly the distance between the baby's and mother's faces during feeding, and studies show that babies have a particular interest in face shapes. They react in the same way to a rudimentary sketch of a face. Studies also show that a baby looks at complicated patterns and shapes in preference to simple ones. If you push your tongue out at a newborn baby as he watches you, he will copy the action — implying that he recognizes a face as something he himself has and responds by using it.

In the weeks to follow, the baby latches on to a face the moment it comes into his vision range. He

The early interest of infants in form and pattern plays an important role in the development of behavior by focusing attention on stimuli that later have adaptive significance. Visual interest in various patterns and shapes was timed while noting reflections in the infants' eyes. Two-month-old infants repeatedly showed preference for the "real" face over the scrambled and the control faces. Importance of pattern rather than color or brightness was illustrated by the infant's preference for a face, a piece of printed matter and a bull's eye rather than the plain red and yellow disks.

scans it from top to bottom and back again to the eyes, and at about the sixth week of life responds to all the smiles that have been fed into him.

From this moment on the baby becomes an increasingly social person. Occasional gurgles turn into a larger range of coos and noises. Deaf children produce the same noises at this age probably because, just as a hearing baby enjoys sounds, a deaf baby enjoys the vibrations in the throat. As time passes social contact becomes increasingly important and the baby recognizes the person who cares for him or her as someone extra-special.

Even as a baby is discovering more about the world around him he is discovering more about his own body: he has found his hands. At birth he had no control over his hands; if they were within range of his mouth he would suck them, but if they moved away he could not bring them back to the mouth. By six weeks he had learned to clasp one hand in another and pull. Only when the hands are fully open do they become the best toy for a baby of this age. A rattle placed in the baby's hand encourages him to follow the noise with his eyes, the first stage of vital hand and eye coordination. Within a few days he begins to watch his hands as they move in front of his face. He experiments with them, tests them by sucking at them (his mouth is still his most accurate sense organ) and links the fingers together. Later he explores the backs of his hands. This crucial stage of coordination can be held back if the baby does not have enough stimulation. Research seems to show that nerve fibers become more efficient at conducting impulses if they are stimulated constantly. The more a baby is given to see, and the more opportunity to do (for example to hit at a soft ball or foil bottlecap hanging above the crib), the quicker and more satisfactory his development will be.

As time passes his hand movements become more refined. At nine months he can oppose his thumb to his fingers, and before the first birthday he can wave from the wrist alone (instead of moving the whole arm), and can point to and pick up something as small as a pea.

Increasing Sociability

The more babies develop, the more feedback they receive from those around them and the more they

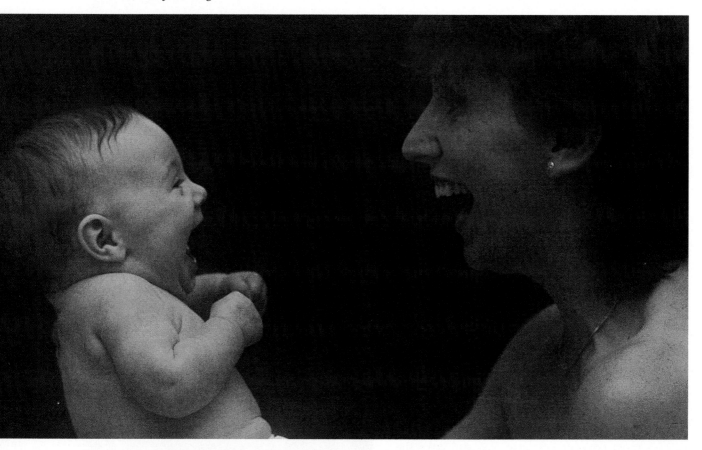

learn. From the moment a baby smiles that first smile, he or she is regarded by the parents as a responsive person. Since the very early days the baby has reacted to speech; by the sixth month he alters vowel sounds by adding consonants, often to produce the "Maa" combination which has lead to the word "Mam" having much the same meaning in many languages. Thanks perhaps to an eager mother repeating this flattering first "word," learning becomes instigation, response and repetition. The baby is a good mimic and can copy the sound of a cough and imitate the babble of adult conversation. He listens with greater concentration, fills in the gaps with answers, and responds to his own name.

It is significant that second and third children often talk more than the first child during the second year of life because they have the constant chatter of a toddler to learn from. It may of course be that a first parent is more inhibited about talking to a baby who shows no obvious response, so that despite the best will in the world the first child never gets as much conversational input as subsequent children.

Toward the end of his first year a baby may use one or two words with meaning. Through the conversations around and addressed to him he has probably picked out a key word, and often finds it easier if a gesture accompanies the word — "Bye-bye" with a wave, or "No" with a shake of the head. The vocabulary may not be large, but the baby can now make himself understood; he is becoming a personality exhibiting emotions of affection or joy, along with jealousy, disappointment and rage.

Developing Immunity

When a baby is born he has enough natural immunity from disease to protect him until he has made his own antibodies. "Passive" immunity is

Benjamin Spock

Friend of the Family

For a whole generation in the United States the surname Spock was synonymous with parental guidance to bringing up children. Published first in 1946, *The Common Sense Book of Baby and Child Care* (later abbreviated to *Baby and Child Care*) by Dr Benjamin McLane Spock sold more copies than any other title.

Spock was born in 1903 in New Haven, Connecticut. He attended Yale University, from which he graduated in 1925, before going on to Columbia University College of Physicians and Surgeons, which granted him his doctorate in 1929. Fifteen years later, the success of his book accorded him considerable fame and status. Another work appeared in 1955 — *Feeding Your Baby and Child* — the year in which Spock took up the position of Professor of Child Development at Western Reserve University (in Cleveland, Ohio). He remained there for twelve years, until 1967, when his political views stirred him to relinquish his professorial post and to assume a prominent public role in protesting against military intervention in Vietnam.

Spock's achievement in the reeducation of an entire generation of American parents to his own ideas of caring for children was extraordinary.

The nineteenth-century values of the turn of the century — strictness and propriety reinforced by a respect for tradition and a fear of punishment — had developed into a regimen of rigidly applied rules regarding what was right and what was not; the rules applied to parents even more than to children. At a time when psychiatry was becoming properly accepted, a large part of each psychiatrist's clientele comprised parents wondering "where they had gone wrong," or whether indeed they were going wrong, in the way they were treating their offspring.

Spock changed all that. His message was one of freedom: enjoy your children, he said; be friends with them. Allow them latitude, and you will have latitude yourselves.

Moreover, his books evolved with the *mores* of the times. As the contraceptive Pill became more available, Spock's calm, wise words increasingly reassured parents that, provided their children were brought up using his approach, excesses of promiscuity and debauchery were unlikely. This was just what his readers wanted to be told. There was also increasing emphasis on advice for one-parent families, and for the child unexpectedly confronted by domestic divorce.

It was not surprising that his work was extremely popular with parents who as children had been rigidly constrained, and who until then had regarded carrying on the tradition as both inevitable and burdensome.

Whether Spock's theories also led to a general climate of indiscipline that encouraged juvenile delinquency — as critics have since alleged — has never been statistically tested. Spock himself, however, was reported at the beginning of the 1980s to have "recanted" on some of his former precepts.

*The result of a few moments'
discomfort while being inoculated
(below left) can provide immunity
to infectious childhood diseases such
as measles, diphtheria and whooping
cough. Occasionally a baby's diaper*
(below right) *can be the cause of a
disorder producing rashes, and
soreness of the buttocks. This too can
be prevented, by scrupulous
attention to washing and drying the
baby, and frequent changes of diaper.*

passed in the blood through the placenta from the
mother and (if the baby is nursed) antibodies are
also present in the mother's milk, particularly the
colostrum produced by the breasts for a couple of
days after birth. This passive immunity has
generally waned by the time the baby is about six
months old, when babies should be immunized
against illnesses such as pertussis (whooping
cough), diphtheria, tetanus, poliomyelitis and
measles, because these can be killer diseases.
Passive immunity persists for longer in some
babies, and parents should seek advice from their
pediatrician.

However, the baby may come into contact with
many other less aggressive viruses and bacteria,
and through this contact build up an immune
system in his own blood. One such virus causes
roseola infantum, which affects children under
three years old and is characterized by small pink
spots and fever for a few days. Most of the viruses

with which a baby comes into contact, however, are those that cause common colds and influenza. These may result in a few days of feeding problems in young babies when their noses are blocked — but each time a baby successfully deals with a virus, it is one more that can be added to the immunity list, never to cause trouble again.

Many ailments affect young babies because their bodies are not sufficiently developed to cope with them. A newborn baby's body may display the struggle with a new environment by various skin troubles manifested as rashes, spots, peeling of skin and blotches. Most of these can quickly and easily be resolved by using some of the mildest of home treatments.

Young babies are prone to regurgitating feeds, some more so than others. This spitting is normal and should not be confused with vomiting caused by infection or, more rarely, obstruction of the digestive tract, either at its upper end or lower down the system. These latter conditions are accompanied by loss of appetite and obvious misery in the baby. Pyloric stenosis causes "projectile vomiting," in which the baby spews feeds three or four feet across the room. This condition, which more usually affects boy babies than girls, results from a congenital thickening in the gut which becomes apparent during the third and fourth week of life. A simple surgical operation can repair the defect. Any persistent vomiting or diarrhea in a young baby can rapidly lead to dehydration, and medical advice should be sought as a matter of urgency.

The End of an Era

By the time a baby reaches the age of two, much of the nervous system is developed. The era of babyhood is really finished and the infant has already attained half adult height. There is still a lot of growing to do and emotional development to take place. But already, by the time the baby is toddling, the parents tend to stop thinking of him or her as a baby. The toddler has personality, displays moods, uses a vocabulary, and makes known likes and dislikes. This young person may still wear a diaper but is definitely part of the family, "one of us," although as yet still standing on the brink of childhood.

Chapter 4

Preschool to Puberty

"She is the child of herself and will be what she is. I am merely the keeper of her temporary helplessness," wrote Laurie Lee as he watched his newborn daughter. By the time a child is two years old, he or she appears to have left most of that helplessness behind; walking, talking, holding a cup, enjoying the company of friends, recognizing people and being an integral part of the small community of the close family. Fundamentally the two-year-old has the same attributes as an eleven- or twelve-year-old — apart from being much smaller. So what factors emerge during the childhood years that make an eleven-year-old child completely different from a pre-school child?

One major factor is independence, in the fullest meaning of the word. Physical independence comes with increasing dexterity and muscular coordination. Emotional independence improves as the child enlarges his (or her) social circle, and attains a greater understanding of the people around him. At first, experiences are restricted to close family members whom the child begins to see as separate individuals, and with this development comes the appearance of various emotions such as sympathy and selflessness. A three-year-old can strive to please an adult in a way a two-year-old would not know how to.

As the years pass and encounters with the world increase, so does the child's ability to judge and reason, to profit by his own experiences. He can personally satisfy the need to learn and no longer depends solely on adults to teach everything. By the time a child reaches the early teenage years, he can face new situations and intelligently adapt behavior to cope with new experiences.

The First Challenge

At the age of two most children still have one major hurdle of neurological development to surmount, and if this is left to the child — instead of being forced on the baby — it is passed more quickly

Gaily flying a kite on a gusty day the little girl in Edgard Wiethase's painting The Kite *epitomizes the independence, abandon and freedom of spirit of childhood. This time of rapid development offers a wealth of experience.*

and easily. It is the full control of the bladder and bowels, the first moral development a child must face — moral because parents have to mold the child's obvious desires until they fit in with what is accepted as normal in society, without offering the child any particular reward other than being pleased. Girls tend to gain bladder control earlier than boys. (Theories to explain this include speculation that the difference in urethral length may be responsible.)

In the past considerable importance was placed on very early training. In many cases the inspiration for such training was a handling reflex present in all young babies: when a diaper is removed and the genital area or the perineal area between the anus and the genital region is touched, urination frequently occurs — as many a parent and pediatrician knows. This reflex also occurs when the baby's buttocks touch the cold rim of a pot, but disappears as a reflex action generally before the first birthday.

Before the age of two, "toilet training" is possible as long as it is clear that at this stage it is the parent — not the baby — who becomes trained to recognize signals that the baby is about to fill the diaper. On these occasions quick action could lead to a "successful" conclusion — but it could equally alarm and irritate a toddler, making subsequent training more difficult.

Some experts point out that by leaving toilet training until after a child's second birthday, he then has the ability to control the situation to a much greater extent, not least because the child has developed some language ability and is able to express his needs more clearly. Beyond the age of two the child is more likely to regard it as a skill that has been learned, not a discipline that has been forced upon him.

A Changing Shape

During the childhood years, growth is slower and more steady than during babyhood or adolescence. A child begins to lose the characteristic chubby, large-headed shape of the baby and becomes longer and slimmer. The proportions of the body change to more closely resemble an adult shape. In fact ninety-five per cent of the skull's growth is complete by the age of ten.

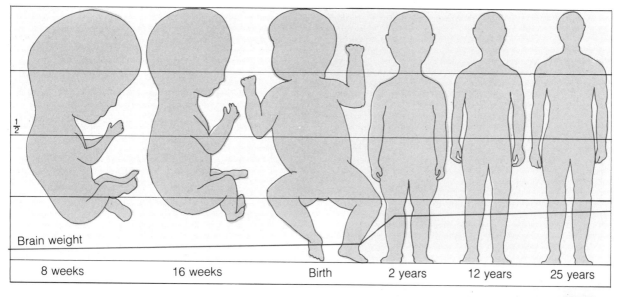

½

Brain weight

| 8 weeks | 16 weeks | Birth | 2 years | 12 years | 25 years |

Children do not grow all the time. Various factors affect growth — in countries north of the equator children put on more weight between the months of October and December than they do at other times of the year, although they grow more in height between the months of April and June. The opposite is true of children living in the southern hemisphere. The reasons for these seasonal variations in growth and weight are not fully understood, but they appear to be part of the rhythmical pattern that is inherent in all forms of life on earth.

Children are taller now than were children of the same age a century ago. Experts feel that this is only partly the result of better nutrition, and that hereditary factors also play an important part. This faster growth rate goes hand in hand with an earlier onset of puberty, with its characteristic accompanying growth spurt.

Illness slows down a child's rate of growth, but a child is able to grow three times faster than normal once well again and any deficit is soon made up. Severe illness, particularly if caused by nutritional problems, can stop growth altogether. If the condition is successfully treated, growth continues again, but several of the long bones retain a narrow band of hardened tissue which may be visible on an X ray.

Growth is controlled by hormones. Growth

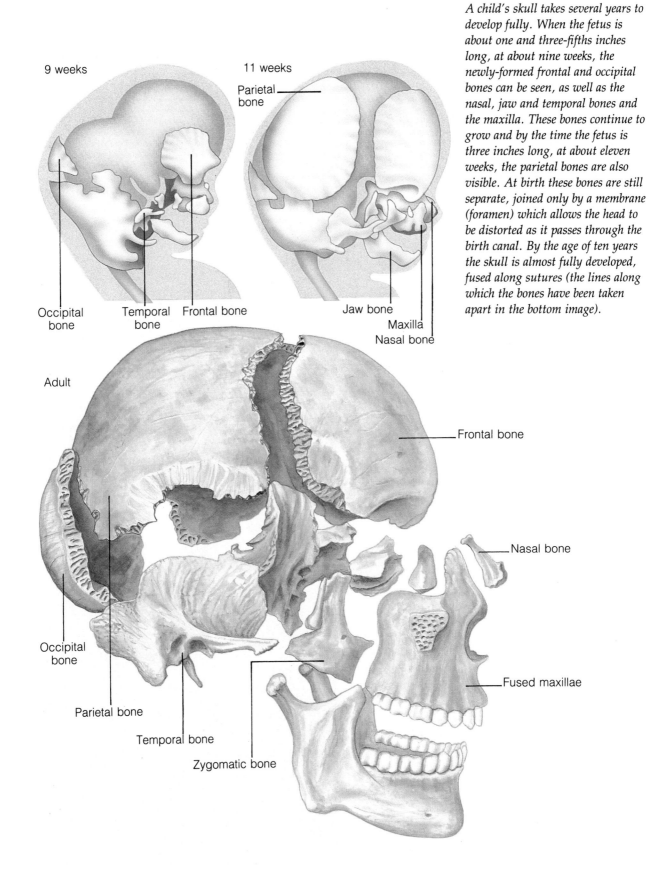

9 weeks

11 weeks

Parietal bone

Occipital bone

Temporal bone

Frontal bone

Jaw bone

Maxilla

Nasal bone

A child's skull takes several years to develop fully. When the fetus is about one and three-fifths inches long, at about nine weeks, the newly-formed frontal and occipital bones can be seen, as well as the nasal, jaw and temporal bones and the maxilla. These bones continue to grow and by the time the fetus is three inches long, at about eleven weeks, the parietal bones are also visible. At birth these bones are still separate, joined only by a membrane (foramen) which allows the head to be distorted as it passes through the birth canal. By the age of ten years the skull is almost fully developed, fused along sutures (the lines along which the bones have been taken apart in the bottom image).

Adult

Frontal bone

Nasal bone

Fused maxillae

Occipital bone

Parietal bone

Temporal bone

Zygomatic bone

*The shape of child's skull (below
left) differs from that of an adult one
(below right) in that a young skull
has short jaw and nasal bones. These
bones give the face its characteristic
soft roundness.*

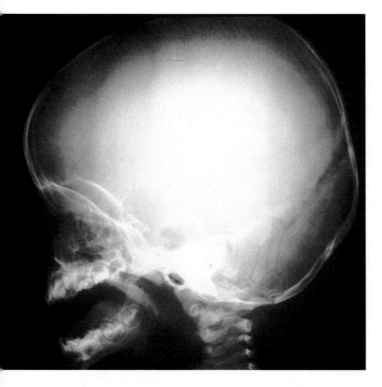

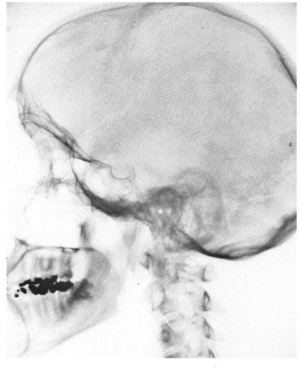

hormone releasing factor (GRF) passes from the hypothalamus in the brain to the rear lobe of the pituitary, the pea-sized endocrine gland that hangs by a stalk from the base of the brain. Thus stimulated, the pituitary releases growth hormone in the form of the protein somatotropin, which is carried in the bloodstream to the liver and kidneys. There it is chemically modified into somatomedin (a polypeptide), and it is thought to be this substance that acts as the growth hormone. In the long bones, for example, it brings about the calcification of cartilage in the growing ends, or epiphyses, of the bones, converting the comparatively soft cartilage into strong hard bone.

Eventually, toward the end of adolescence, growth hormone inhibiting factor (GIF) from the hypothalamus slows down and then stops the release of somatotropin by the pituitary. If this "switching off" mechanism fails, the individual continues to grow – a condition known as gigantism. Continued production of growth hormone after adulthood causes acromegaly, a disorder in which the bones of the hands and face become lumpy and overgrown. If, on the other hand, the pituitary fails

to produce enough growth hormone during childhood, dwarfism results. Children who appear to be much too tall or much too small for their age can be medically examined, and treatment initiated to correct the imbalance of growth hormone.

"Normal" children vary a great deal. Often too much emphasis is put on the amount a child should eat. Growth slows during the childhood years and appetite varies with changing patterns of growth. A happy energetic child is probably incapable of eating less than he needs — problems of this nature can occur during adolescence, but they do not manifest themselves during childhood. A malnourished child may be listless, saving all the energy for growth alone, leaving little or none over for play.

A child who has access to a healthful, balanced diet, and is not pressurized to eat any specific type of foods — whether those of a strict vegetarian diet or of the "fast food" culture — generally consumes all he needs to grow and stay healthy. The eating pattern may appear erratic, but is generally health-sustaining. Many years ago researchers proved that babies as young as four

months old have an inbuilt ability to conduct their own nutrition along the lines recommended by experts. A human being probably no more needs to be "taught" to eat the correct foods than does a baby turtle which hatches and embarks on life at sea without ever seeing the mother turtle.

Being the correct weight is an aspect of growth related to diet. A slightly underweight child is usually just as healthy as a child of average weight, and commonly comes from thin stock. Organic disorders such as tuberculosis, the chronic digestive disorder celiac disease, or asthma may cause wasting, but skinniness is usually a natural tendency. Some children put weight on only during the summer months; others only during school vacations. In any case, the major problem in Western countries today is children who overeat, not those who eat too little.

Obesity is a condition more difficult to deal with. Overweight parents tend to have overweight children, and recent evidence points more to the passing on of a metabolic disorder, as opposed to bad eating habits, by the parents, although often it is a combination of these factors that causes the problem. Fatness should be checked early because fat children tend to become progressively less energetic, which worsens the problem, in that the child has a decreasing chance of voluntarily taking part in vigorous physical activity and thus "burning off" the unwanted fat.

A toddler needs little encouragement to run and use a new-found skill, but older children have less need for such mindless exercise and may require encouragement to expend energy. They want someone to run with or play ball with; they need the extra incentive such as a bicycle or roller skates to burn off the calories. A fat child also requires guidance away from eating sugary and fatty snacks, but this must be presented tactfully because obesity in an older child is almost impossible to control

The amount of fat a child carries on his or her body is dependent on heredity, general state of health and access to an adequate and correctly balanced diet. The Danakil girl from northern Kenya (above right) is much thinner than her European counterpart (above left).

unless the child himself has the necessary incentive and motivation to achieve such control.

Adult Teeth

Permanent teeth begin to emerge through the gums at about the age of six. The first may be the four molars at the back (which some adults assume to be milk teeth because the child does not have to lose teeth to make way for them). The next to erupt are usually at the front on the lower jaw. A milk tooth becomes progressively wobbly over a space of six to eight weeks until it falls out, revealing the tip of the adult tooth below.

The permanent teeth then erupt in approximately the same order in which the milk teeth emerged. At first the new teeth look disproportionate in size and darker than the remaining small milk teeth, but the child's face gradually grows to accommodate them. Initially they have an exaggerated rough cutting edge, but this too gradually alters through

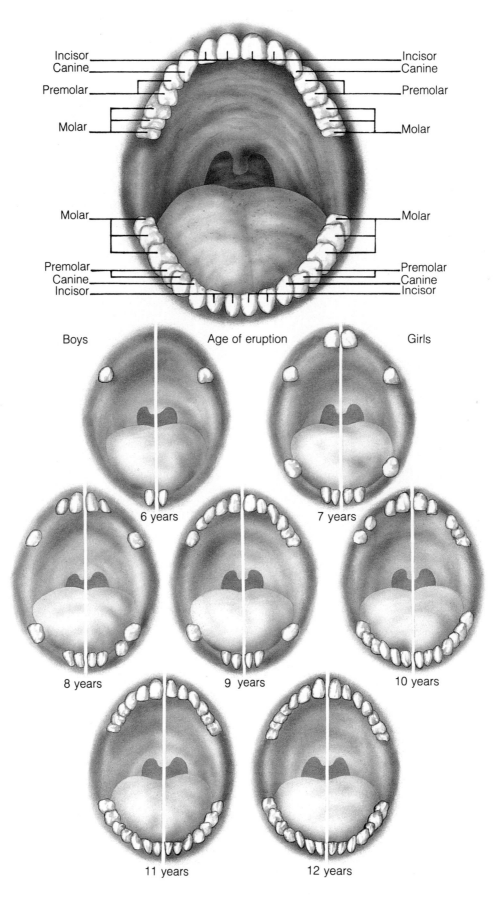

Incisor — — Incisor
Canine — — Canine
Premolar — — Premolar

Molar — — Molar

Molar — — Molar

Premolar — — Premolar
Canine — — Canine
Incisor — — Incisor

Boys   Age of eruption   Girls

6 years   7 years

8 years   9 years   10 years

11 years   12 years

80

The average ages at which boys and girls develop their permanent teeth vary slightly, but most begin at about six years, and all except the wisdom teeth have erupted by about the age of twelve. The chart (left)

shows the ages at which different permanent teeth erupt — boys' teeth on the left, girls' on the right. To preserve the teeth good dental care is essential with regular visits to a dentist (below).

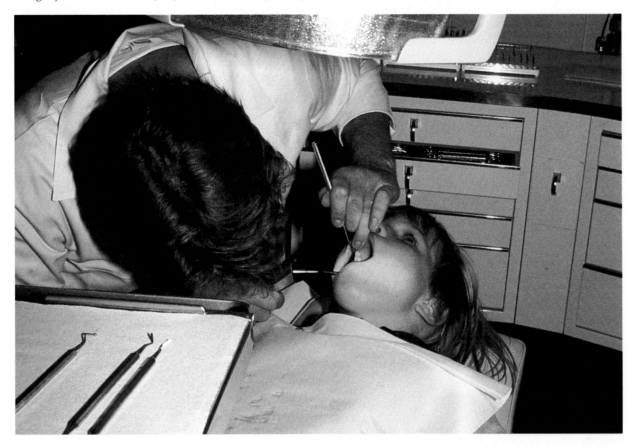

use to give a normal adult smooth-edged tooth. Overcrowding is a common problem when permanent teeth begin to emerge. The usual cause is a small jaw trying to accommodate too many teeth. If humans are products of natural selection, the fact that, unlike a sheep, we can survive without our teeth probably accounts for this piece of poor design in our anatomy. Whatever the reason, overcrowded teeth need extra care because if the vertical and horizontal alignment is disrupted, food and bacteria can become caught in the gaps. Regular visits to the dentist or orthodontist can solve many potential problems before they become serious. An orthodontist may delay treatment until the age of ten or more.

As with every other aspect of a child's development, good teeth are a combination of inherited traits and external factors such as diet and good oral hygiene. A diet rich in vitamins A, C and D and low in sugar is important from birth, because the teeth

are developing in the jaw throughout that time. Some experts believe that in respect of decay sugar is the sole culprit, although others believe that a range of carbohydrates can be broken down into sugary elements.

Before the age of seven, few children clean every tooth surface adequately every time, so parental supervision is often advised to make sure that cleaning is done correctly. Disclosing tablets can be chewed to show up areas of debris and plaque. When the color (blue or red) has been cleaned away, the teeth themselves are completely clear of plaque. Fluoridation of drinking-water supplies by local water departments also assists in the prevention of tooth decay.

Developing Coordination

Children seem to have an unlimited ability to learn new skills, but just how much can a child achieve through special training and encouragement? Are

The ability to learn varies from child to child and depends on hereditary factors as well as teaching. Some children learn remarkably fast, such as the composer Wolfgang Amadeus Mozart, who amazed his contemporaries by composing music for the harpsichord and the violin before the age of five.

limits of ability preset by heredity or can they be overruled by environment? The answer has to be that both factors affect coordination.

Most three-year-olds can pedal a tricycle; a few can balance on a bicycle at the age of four; and most children are competent cyclists by the time they are seven or eight. Some children develop coordination at an extraordinarily precocious age — the four-year-old Mozart mastered the hand coordination necessary to play the violin to a remarkably high standard. But often a child is held back by other more complex factors.

In gymnastics, for example, children peak before they reach puberty, but not long before. A twelve-year-old gymnast must, after all, be more efficient than a three-year-old one. Stature and physical strength are significant, as is also maturing emotional strength in the field of sport. But it is the stimulation of the nerve pathways through training, plus the physical maturation of the nerves themselves that add to the conductivity of impulses within the brain, and these in turn are responsible, to a large degree, for improvements in hand and eye coordination.

Unless held back by fear or insecurity, children tend to push themselves to the limits of their abilities; throughout childhood they are a mass of energy and exploration. They climb trees, they become increasingly interested in sport and other physical activities, they test their bodies under unusual conditions — for example, in water when they learn to swim. They experiment with gravity by swinging, jumping from heights, or using a seesaw. They master motion to its fullest degree, running, chasing, ducking and catching one another. Every physical activity teaches the brain about the body — they learn the incredible things they can expect from their physiques and they use them to the full.

In many activities a child needs to find his or her own limitations: how far is safe to jump, how high is safe to climb. Other activities are controlled by adults with consideration toward the child's stage of development. For example, a child under the age of eight should not use a skateboard without adult supervision. Neither should a child under the age of ten be regarded as wholly reliable at road safety. Before ten, a child cannot judge speed and distance

Pieter Breughel's painting of children's games in the sixteenth century (above) records in marvelous detail the energy, imagination and coordinated motion of children, characteristics which are seen today in exactly the same games. However, new toys and sports devised as technology advances do change children's activities in some ways — an example of this is the skateboard (right). In developing a child's judgment of speed, gravity and balance, skateboarding teaches children what their bodies can and cannot do.

Children have to be controlled in some activities because their judgment and knowledge are not well enough developed for them to manage on their own. Activities in the kitchen provide many excellent learning situations, often especially enjoyable because a parent may be involved. Children learn not only about food and its preparation, but also about timing, measurement and planning ahead.

of vehicles and so must be regarded as potentially unsafe on a cycle or even on foot.

So much for gross coordination, but many other areas have to be tried and tested. A child's ability to concentrate increases during these years and gives an opportunity for the development of fine hand movements. Children learn to sew, to paint and draw, to play a musical instrument, to manipulate pastry for cooking, to build construction kits, to use a pair of scissors and to write.

In respect of the ability to write it is significant that children who suffer from the disorder of communication known as type B dyslexia lack also an ability to coordinate hand and eye movement. They tend to be clumsy and have little or no sense of orientation, even to the extent of being unable to imagine the relationship of one room to another within their own home. Children with the less serious type A dyslexia primarily have problems with learning to read and write. Much of the successful modern treatment of the condition is aimed at recreating the process of hand and eye coordination learning that a normal child goes through alone.

"Draw a man" is one of the standard tests used by pediatricians to assess the stage of a child's intellectual development. It is interesting to note that a child draws figures from about the age of two-and-a-half to three without any instruction from an adult. From then on the figures become more complicated but the emphasis for the first five or six years is placed strongly on the face, which is usually drawn out of proportion to the rest of the body. Gradually the child adds detail — eyes, nose, hair, clothing — but the process is one of drawing a shape then recognizing an image. The adult ability to look at an object then translate the image onto paper comes much later.

Reading and writing are learned in much the same way; recognition first, application second. A child recognizes his name from the shape the letters form as a group. Once the child is a proficient reader, he returns to this system of reading, but before then must learn a library of word shapes in conjunction with a phonetic understanding of separate letters. This seems a daunting task even for the receptive brain of a child, but research shows that in ordinary everyday English just

Children's skills and abilities become more varied as their nervous and muscular systems develop. At the age of about two, most children are able to construct small towers with blocks. A year later they can dress themselves. By the age of three they have enough manual dexterity to perform relatively difficult tasks, such as eating a boiled egg (right). Coordination is refined enough at the age of four to play ball games. At about five years of age, dexterity and visual perception have progressed so that a square can be drawn fairly accurately. The ability to concentrate and learn increases with age, and at six most children can read without help. The sense of time develops, so that by about seven, they can tell the time. Balance and judgment of speed improve, so that by eight most children can ride a bicycle. A sense of comradeship and responsibility is usually developed by age ten, and this is often apparent in the games children play, as Winslow Homer's painting Snap the Whip (above) shows well.

Maria Montessori

Toward a Kinder Kindergarten

For the last fifty years at least, in most Western societies schooling has been based much more on actually interesting the pupil enough to achieve maximum potential at his or her own volition. This has meant the introduction of new teaching techniques, of different teaching aids corresponding to the tenets of child psychology, and above all, of a new atmosphere in which each individual is encouraged to discover his or her own capabilities.

The person more responsible than anyone else for this introduction was Maria Montessori.

She was born in Chiaravalle, near the eastern coast of central Italy, in August 1870. The first woman in her country to graduate in medicine at the University of Rome—which she did in 1894 — she was then appointed assistant doctor at the psychiatric clinic there. And it was over the following five years that she began to turn her mind to the improvement of educational standards by altering teaching methods. Her initial work was with retarded children, and was so successful that in 1899 she was appointed Director of the State Orthophrenic School in Rome, lecturing also at the University. The Chair in anthropology was hers

between the years 1904 and 1908.

She opened her first *casa dei bambini*, or "children's home," in 1907. Consisting only of a set of rooms off a courtyard in the slums of Rome, it represented a new form of kindergarten for three- to six-year-olds. The methods of instruction that had been applied to the retarded children were now applied to normal children—and with equal success. In particular, the new role of the teacher was to remain relatively in the background, advising and enthusing rather than merely disciplining the children.

Children were quickly discovered to have far more learning potential than had previously been imagined, and to concentrate better on what they were doing, too, if their hearts were in it. Furthermore, the new method encouraged initiative and self-motivation, and allowed the children also to proceed at virtually their own pace.

Dr. Maria Montessori's fame spread, as did her methods; many other Montessori schools were established. She was allowed little time herself to get on with practical application, however—for the following four decades she toured throughout Europe, Asia and North America giving lectures and inaugurating teacher-training programs. Simultaneously she was writing accounts of her system and its successes.

Recognition of her efforts came from many countries. In her own, however—although she had been appointed government inspector of all Italian schools in 1922—the rise to power of the Fascists obliged her to emigrate. She spent some time first in Spain and then Sri Lanka (then Ceylon), before domiciling herself in Holland.

It was in that country that she died—in May 1952 at Noordwijk aan Zee.

twelve different words are repeated so often as to make up one whole quarter of the words we read, one hundred form half, and three hundred form almost three-quarters. Many systems to teach reading are based on this, because early success motivates a child to read.

Language and Original Thought

One of the most significant differences between a toddler and a child is the increased ability to communicate. A toddler usually communicates in an emotional way, and parents generally communicate with a toddler through actions, even if they are accompanied by talk. A child, however, uses his enlarged language skills to control situations, and an adult uses the child's augmented intellect to encourage sociable behavior.

The child is increasingly in control of his own destiny. He can discuss and reason with an adult if he wants something; he can explain his actions, and excuse his mistakes. In the right home environment, childhood is regarded as the most mutually satisfying era of growing up. The child has left behind the frustrations of being a victim to a body and mind unable to encompass the desires of independence, but has not yet reached the stage of asserting that independence with the vehemence that typifies adolescence. He is still a child. He still needs the firm foundation of a secure family from which to set out to discover the world about him, and does not resent the emotional ties that the family have over him.

A child has rights at every age, but it is throughout childhood that these rights are often eroded because a child's desires conflict with those of adults. For example, researchers have discovered that children who are smacked as a punishment often remember only the smack, not the reason they were punished. The blow is so humiliating that their anger wipes away any chance of remorse. In Sweden the government is so certain of the importance of these rights that hitting a child under any circumstances is a prosecutable offense and regarded also as psychic assault. Raising a voice in anger toward a child is regarded similarly. The rest of the Western world walks an uneasy tightrope between the extremes of strict discipline on the one hand and total freedom on the other.

Corporal punishment and violence toward children is regarded increasingly as bearing potentially serious long-term psychological effects, similar to other forms of physical assault. This attitude is reflected in some countries in legislation that makes hitting a child a punishable offence.

87

A compromise is probably best. An over-disciplined child has trouble reaching moral decisions alone, and it can be dangerously naive to assume that parental control overcomes this deficiency. But at the same time a child has to learn to fit into society at large because we are a sociable species and only by learning discipline can self-discipline be achieved. During school years children hate to be different, even to the extent of disliking unusual names that parents have chosen for them. They need to be like their contemporaries and may be ostracized with uncompromising cruelty if they are too different in their behavior or appearance.

Once a child is equipped with a rich language, parents should recognize a child's right to discuss (as opposed to argue), to comment (not answer back), and to reach a compromise (rather than making the parent lose face). If a parent can retain an understanding of this, the child retains confidence and respect in himself as a person in addition to respect for the parent. Through this relationship a child brings back new ideas and original thoughts, displays a sense of humor and provides the joy of living alongside someone with an individual personality. "In this role," wrote Laurie Lee, "I see her leading me back to my beginnings, reopening rooms I'd locked and forgotten, stirring the dust in my mind by re-asking the big questions . . ."

Gender Identity

Recent evidence seems to show that babies are far better at recognizing the differences between boy and girl infants than are most adults. Experiments are based on the fact that people tend to observe members of their own sex more than those of the opposite sex. A woman watching a movie looks at the female characters more than the males; the opposite is true of a man watching a movie. This is probably because we identify with the character most like ourselves.

Babies generally do the same, and researchers have come to realize that even when key identifying features such as long hair or modes of dress are missing, baby girls still watch baby girls on film more than they watch baby boys. They seem to recognize them because their movements are

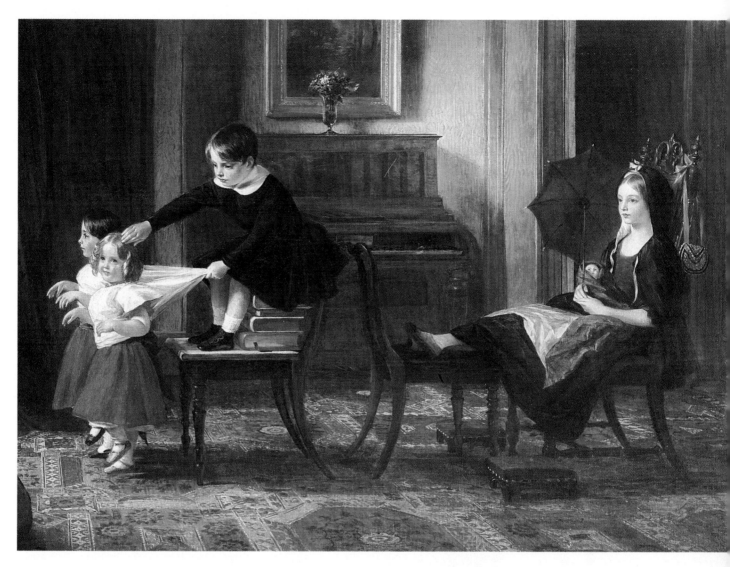

different — boy toddlers tend to move from the shoulders, girl toddlers from the hips.

Whatever personal opinions people have about gender identification and conditioning during childhood, there is little doubt that boys and girls differ outwardly from a very early age. They do not, of course, differ in their ability to achieve.

Children enjoy role-playing; they enjoy dressing up and taking part in imaginative play. This feature is often reflected in gender identification, and much controversy rages over the subject. Most small boys see their mothers doing many more things around the home than they see their fathers doing, so why should they not mimic their mothers' daily chores? Equally, most girls are just as likely to witness their mothers using a power tool or carrying out routine automobile maintenance, so why should they choose to mimic the acts of caring and homebuilding above others?

This attitude cannot be solely attributed to

This charming nineteenth-century painting Children playing at Coach and Horses, *by Charles Robert Leslie, depicts the vivid imagination children exercise in their games, and also notes the details children associate with adults. The young girl sits regally in her "carriage," cradling a doll and carrying a parasol. The young boy drives the coach on, gently urging the "horses" forward.*

environment; something in the different physical and mental makeup of each sex probably plays a part. The fact that the mother is usually with both the boy and the girl child most of the time may account for the fact that girls tend to identify with their mothers before boys identify with their fathers. Some psychologists believe that girls have a mature empathy at an early age because of the dilemma they find themselves in within their families. From the moment a young girl realizes the difference between her mother and her father, she strives to please her father. According to this school of thought, she becomes confused in middle childhood because she wishes her mother was not there so that she could have sole rights to her father, but she also loves and needs her mother.

It is this early concealment of feeling that these psychologists believe equips women with skillful techniques to handle emotions. Most little girls can manipulate their fathers quite effectively, and if through this relationship a girl is made to feel loved and valued, her confidence in herself in future life is assured.

The situation should theoretically be easier for a boy. A girl's first love can become her rival, whereas a boy's first love is often his first sexual love. Unfortunately, reaction to this emotion causes him just as many problems. According to some psychologists, many of the misconceptions men retain about women in adult life stem from insensitive handling of what is known as the "oedipal" phase. This theory postulates that at about the age of five, a boy is sexually interested in his mother. If the reaction to this interest is displeasure or, worse, punishment, his lasting impression may be that women are sexless and the boy enters a world of men and excludes women. These feelings come very much to the fore at the end of childhood but before adolescence has begun. Boys exclude girls from their games; they tend to form gangs and put women down in conversation.

When all the consequences of the conflicting emotions that beset a growing child are considered, it may seem incredible that anyone reaches adulthood as an adjusted person. But it should be remembered that each stage is within the realms of normality. Children are resilient and adaptable,

Jacques Monod and François Jacob

The Cellular Switch

Together, Jacques Lucien Monod and François Jacob formulated a theory on how metabolism – and by inference growth and development – within cells might be controlled by genes – a hypothesis that has since been proved correct in respect of a large number of cells.

Monod was born in Paris in February 1910. He graduated at Paris University in 1931 and gained his doctorate there ten years later, after in the meantime becoming Assistant Professor of Zoology at the Pasteur Institute. From 1945 to 1953 he collaborated with Jacob (and with André Lwoff) on the work that led eventually to a Nobel Prize for all three. At the end of that time he held senior appointments at both the Institute and the University; he became Director of the Pasteur Institute in 1971.

Jacob is ten years younger, born in June 1920 in Nancy. He too was educated in Paris, graduating in medicine in 1947 and gaining his doctorate in 1954. Of the partnership with Monod, he was the geneticist whereas Monod was essentially a biochemist. Since that time, he too has held senior posts at both the Pasteur Institute and Paris University.

Cell replication is responsible for the growth of every organism. Many cells are

equally responsible for the organism's metabolism (and thus its total welfare) through the production of enzymes or other proteins. But cells are not always replicating, nor are they endlessly producing proteins. Part of the intention behind the experiments undertaken by Monod and Jacob was to discover the mechanism that "switches" the various processes on or off. Genes had ultimately to be responsible, because the production of each enzyme is regulated by a gene.

Proteins are made by ribosomes in the cell, and the "instructions" for their formation are delivered from the DNA in the chromosomes via a molecule that carries the necessary genetic information – called messenger RNA. Monod and Jacob proposed that at one point along the chromosome there might be a "repressor" gene which produced a substance that then acted on a lower "operator" gene (normally partly responsible for protein synthesis) to stop the instructions (messenger RNA) from ever being sent, so that no protein would be formed. The group of genes headed by the operator gene (and thus blocked) Monod and Jacob called the "operon" – and it is now known that a system of this kind is indeed operative in organisms such as bacteria.

In May 1976, five years after the publication of his successful book *Chance and Necessity* – a biochemist's look at evolution – Jacques Monod died. François Jacob remains closely connected with the Pasteur Institute.

Japanese children in a Tokyo kindergarten are taught how to use computers at an early age through the medium of computer games. Computers are thought to speed learning, and most schoolchildren learn how to use them at some time.

and not all stress is harmful — they have to be able to face stress in later life. In order to develop a full personality, however, they must retain their confidence in themselves, and it is this factor that should be uppermost in every parent's mind throughout a child's upbringing.

The Modern World

Children of the 1930s were warned that the cinema would stop them ever wanting to read a book; children of the 1950s were warned that the radio would destroy conversation; children of the 1960s were told that television would destroy their ability to entertain themselves. In the 1980s the computer is the defendant in the case against the intellectual suppressor.

Most parents and teachers alike accept that children can learn a great deal from television if the subject is handled with care. Children between the ages of three and five can concentrate on television for only about fifteen minutes, but even when

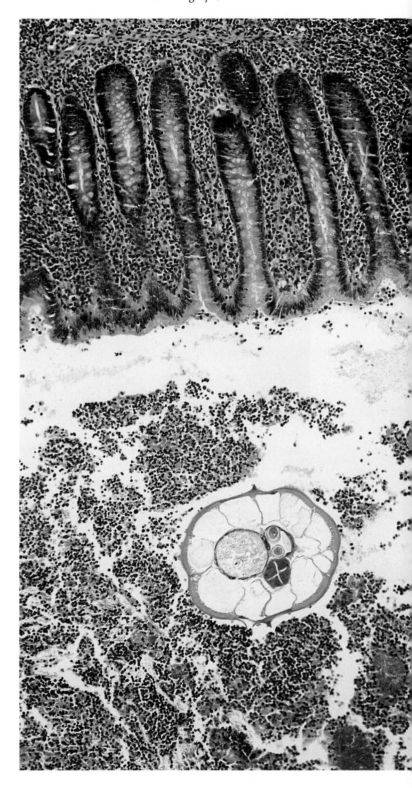

Threadworm, or pinworm, is picked up by children from house dust, contaminated clothing, or from objects they put in their mouths. The worm lays its eggs (the round object in this micrograph) near the anus.

concentrating a child can be confused by television techniques such as close-ups or quick editing from one subject to another. Young children should not be put in a situation in which television is an alternative to parental communication; it should be an adjunct to it. If father watches the television with the child, for instance, he can explain and talk over subjects afterward.

Parental guidance on television viewing is important in older age groups as well. Children seem to retain more knowledge from films about topics such as wild animals and unfamiliar parts of the world than they do by looking at still photographs or reading about them. Research has also shown that a child's vocabulary is often better among television watchers before the age of ten. But children seldom talk to a television, even if they are watching a program that invites them to do so. For this reason, a discussion with an adult after watching a program can make the child's experience far more fulfilling.

Similarly, the computer can be used or abused. It should not be another "babysitter," but the new technology and magic of controlling the image that appears on a screen often stimulates children to achieve earlier reading abilities, because this is the only language they can use to "talk" to a computer. Like cinema, radio and television, the computer is here to stay, and so it is best that a child learns a respect for the avenues this new "toy" will open.

Common Childhood Disorders

The most common reason for hospitalization and visits to the doctor in the age group three to six is an accident resulting in cuts, abrasions or broken bones. It is a very physical age, and minor accidents are one of its consequences, although bone-breaking tends apparently to run in families. It seems that some children inherit tougher, more flexible bones and survive unharmed accidents that would cause a fracture in another child.

A preschool child may seem to have a period of trouble-free health (perhaps when he or she has dealt with any germs that have been contracted). But starting school inevitably means encountering new germs and may herald a time of seemingly endless coughs and colds, earache and running noses. Along with these more common disorders

come some of the infectious diseases likely to affect children simply because they are so infectious.

Chickenpox is caused by the same virus that causes shingles in adults, the *Herpes zoster* virus. A child becomes mildly feverish; at first a rash of small red spots appears over the skin and in the mouth. The spots turn into bubbles of clear fluid (vesicles) which then burst and crust over during the next few days. The spots tend to be very itchy. Occasionally a spot contracts a secondary bacterial infection, and may go on to form a small circular scar, although otherwise chickenpox is a mild illness. In adulthood the disease is more uncomfortable, resembling a bad influenza attack.

Mumps (parotitis) may also affect children around school age, but is uncommon in younger children. The first signs are pain under the jaw when the child eats. This occurs because the mumps virus causes inflammation of the salivary glands, and pain is felt when the child salivates. Shortly afterward the child has a raised temperature and the parotid glands on one side of the face swell. A few days later the other side may become swollen, as may an area beneath the jaw. The swellings in the face and neck may totally alter the child's appearance.

Some problems of childhood produce in parents a more unfavorable reaction than others. One such is bedwetting. Many children are not reliably dry at night before the age of five, and some not until the age of seven (even though others may be dry from the moment they lose their daytime diaper). If a child is generally dry but starts a phase of being wet again, it may be the result of an emotional upset, such as a move of home or a parent's absence for a time. If an organic cause is suspected, medical advice can be sought, although a relaxed approach is more likely to be successful.

Another subject that raises more problems for the parent than for the child is pinworm (threadworm) infestation. Children spend a lot of time putting things in their mouths, especially their fingers. The pinworm lays eggs around the anus at night and the resultant itching can be a cause of bedwetting. The eggs become lodged beneath the child's fingernails and are recycled through the bowel. Treatment is simple and swift, but all the family must take a dose of the medication that kills the pinworms, because they may have also become unwitting hosts. So there is nothing shameful about having worms.

A child with parents who suffer from allergies such as hay fever is quite likely to be allergic too. It may not be the same allergy — it could be asthma or eczema — but the child's body reacts unfavorably to foreign proteins.

One cause of asthma is an allergy to the house dust mite, invisible to the naked eye but indigenous to inhabited houses. The mite lives on the scales of dead skin which humans are constantly shedding and which are abundant in bedding and soft furnishings. A child's asthma can be controlled by adopting a regime of scrupulous cleanliness, including frequent vacuuming of the mattress and changing of bedlinen.

Children may develop allergies to particular types of food — dairy products, strawberries, coconut, fish or shellfish for instance. They erupt in a violently itchy rash known as urticaria (hives), which fades in a few hours. Occasionally a large white lump appears on the face or genitals.

The prognosis for allergic children is good. Allergies tend to alter pattern and intensity as the child grows and may disappear altogether when the child reaches adulthood.

A great deal of research has recently been carried out into more bizarre forms of food allergy. Migraine headaches, which often begin around the age of seven or eight, may, in rare cases, be triggered by foods such as chocolate or cheese. But researchers are now looking at much more wholesome foods such as wheat, milk and eggs, which some scientists suspect can cause a type of "asthma of the bowel" and give a pattern of seemingly unconnected symptoms. (It is the wheat protein gluten, for example, to which children who have celiac disease are intolerant.) Children may also be affected by color additives or preservatives in processed foods. If such allergies are suspected, medical advice should be sought because it is useless to prohibit the eating of certain foods by a healthy child just in case he or she might develop this type of allergy. In any case the research is still in its infancy.

Troubles Ahead

The pre-adolescent phase starts for girls any time after the age of eight and for boys usually after the age of ten. Hormones within the body begin a slow increase in activity, and although there are no external signs at first, small emotional signals warn that adolescence is not far away. For example an uninhibited little girl suddenly bans her father and brothers from the bathroom; a gregarious boy suddenly becomes self-conscious.

Difficult times may lie ahead for child and family alike, but easing the stress depends on what has gone before, not what comes after. Successful relationships during childhood in conjunction with a stable family background are the keys to steering a somewhat turbulent adolescent through to adulthood. Changes in family attitude now are too late; the rollercoaster is at the top of the run and the rails have been set to guide its course. It may be a bumpy ride — exhilarating at times, terrifying at others — but with a firm structure beneath no one is going to come to harm.

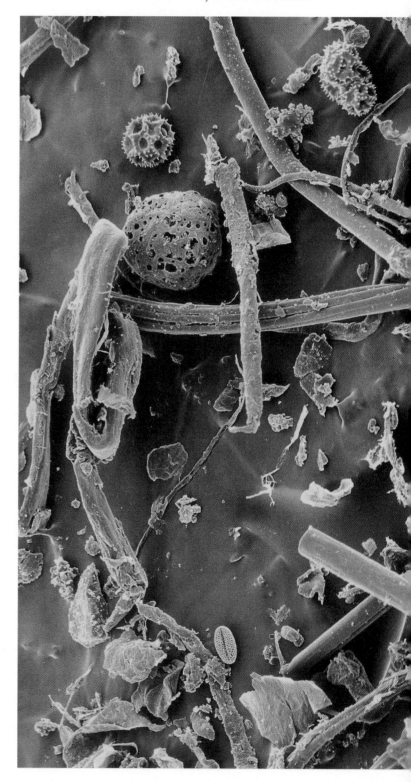

The dust found in homes contains synthetic and natural fibers, pollen, soot particles, and human skin debris, as shown in this micrograph. This dust attracts dust mites, a common cause of asthma in children.

Chapter 5

The Turbulent Teens

Like all stages of growth and development, adolescence has its physical and its psychological aspects. But, more than at any other stage, these two aspects are interwoven, with behavioral manifestations often dominant. The transition from childhood into adulthood bears many similarities to the transition from babyhood to childhood although, unlike the toddler with temper tantrums, the "lounging adolescent" may seem less forgivable simply because he or she is so near adulthood.

A toddler wants independence in the world, but is generally afraid of it and needs a parent nearby. Frustrations may produce uncontrollable and frightening emotions that the child cannot understand. An adolescent is not so very different. The need for independence sometimes fights against self-consciousness. Many teenagers seem self-assured, even pompous, priggish and aggressive, but such behavior may hide genuine fears and worries. An adolescent needs eventually to break loose, to become released from the influence of parents, but parents may be the only people who love in spite of everything — they are someone to come home to. Many adolescents replace childish temper tantrums with more mature intellectual tantrums.

Added to these personal problems may be difficulties within the family itself. A toddler usually has young parents, often still establishing their careers, whereas the parents of teenagers may be facing a midlife crisis of their own, making them, perhaps, not the most sympathetic of companions. The mother or father may have to cope with the loss of one of their own parents; the mother may be seeking other opportunities now that her time is not taken up fully by the children; the father may have career worries; the marriage may not be as stable as in the early years. Whatever the reasons, the parental attitude may sometimes be that a teenager should be old enough to sort out his or her own problems.

Brazen, jazzy and self-conscious, this poster for a motorcycle magazine captures the spirit of adolescence — featuring the glinting chrome of motorbikes, music on tap from a jukebox, the camaraderie of the soda bar, sport, an obsession with appearance, and the dawning awareness of sexuality.

The celebration of a girl's first menstruation in Bali (below) is a public acknowledgment of her entry into adulthood, and through the ritual she is taught how she is expected to behave as an adult.

Many teenagers are unsettled by the apparent split in adults' expectations of them, which they may regard as polarized. At one extreme young people are apparently treated as ignorant, irresponsible children, and at the other they are pressurized to take on serious, adult moral responsibilities. Examples are those thought old enough to fight for their country (bottom left), but who are not considered old enough to vote.

Western culture puts added strain on the adolescent. In many unwesternized societies the onset of puberty heralds the start of a system of established social *mores* through which each adolescent passes. The teenager knows what is expected — for example, a tribal group may be told of a girl's sexual maturity and availability for marriage. The shifting, changing society of the West offers no such structure, however. Many teenagers feel alienated from the adult world, yet they are expected to conform to it. The law states that they have individual responsibilities, but the age at which these start differs. A twelve-year-old is classed as an adult on an airline ticket; and in most states a sixteen-year-old may be considered adult enough to drive a car. From the age of the onset of puberty sexual interests are high, yet in most Westernized society an adolescent has no guiltless outlet for these strong urges even though he or she is not expected to marry until into the twenties.

It is hardly surprising then that some adolescents, at the peak of intellectual and sexual development, feel frustrated, angry and confused by the pressures and responsibilities that seem to impinge on them from every side.

On the Brink of Adulthood

The onset of puberty is brought about by increasing levels of sex hormones in the body. In girls it starts on average two years earlier than in boys. For both, the levels of hormones begin increasing before any external signs appear, and the timing of the start of puberty varies enormously between individuals. The age of menarche (the first period) in girls has in Western societies been dropping steadily for many years, from an average age once of seventeen to the present age of about twelve. Hereditary factors play an important part, as do some aspects which are less immediately understandable, such as individual body weight.

Consider first the onset of puberty in girls. The first external sign is the change in one or both nipples into what is known as the breast "bud." The pigmented area around the nipple (the areola) enlarges and a small mound appears. This can happen at any time between the ages of eight and thirteen, but the average age is eleven.

The twenty-eight-day menstrual cycle starts with the menstrual flow, which consists of the degenerated endometrium that normally lines the uterus. During bleeding, which lasts about five days, a follicle starts to develop in the ovary. By the fourteenth day it is ripe and bursts, releasing an egg (ovulation). Just before ovulation estrogen is secreted, which causes the endometrium to thicken. The empty follicle becomes the corpus luteum and produces hormones which build up the endometrium further. If the egg is not fertilized or does not implant, the corpus luteum degenerates, and the endometrium deteriorates.

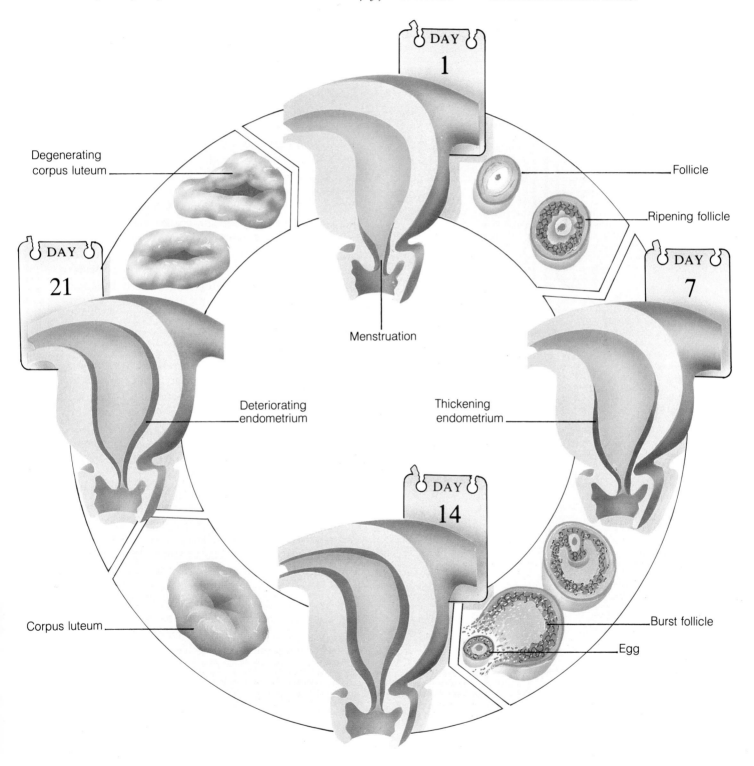

DAY 1

Degenerating corpus luteum

Follicle

Ripening follicle

DAY 21

DAY 7

Menstruation

Deteriorating endometrium

Thickening endometrium

DAY 14

Corpus luteum

Burst follicle

Egg

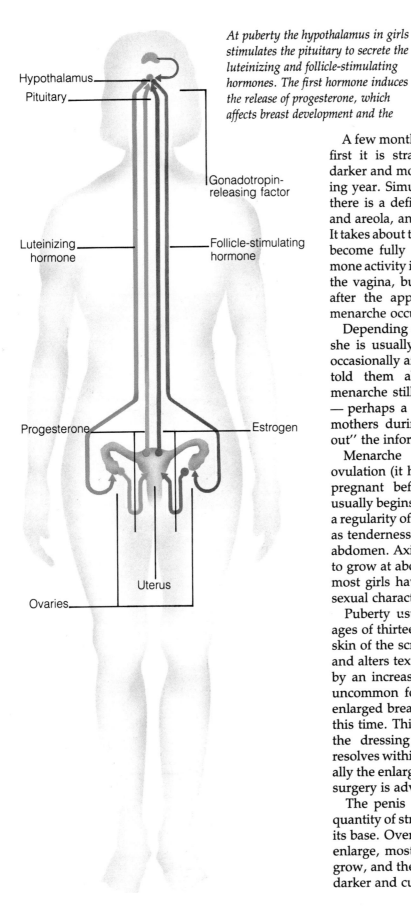

Hypothalamus

Pituitary

Gonadotropin-releasing factor

Luteinizing hormone

Follicle-stimulating hormone

Progesterone

Estrogen

Uterus

Ovaries

At puberty the hypothalamus in girls stimulates the pituitary to secrete the luteinizing and follicle-stimulating hormones. The first hormone induces the release of progesterone, which affects breast development and the menstrual cycle, and the second causes the release of estrogen, which develops female sexual characteristics. The blood levels of these hormones are fed back to and controlled by the hypothalamus.

A few months later pubic hair begins to grow. At first it is straight and unpigmented, becoming darker and more abundant throughout the following year. Simultaneously the breasts enlarge until there is a definite distinction between the nipple and areola, and the contour of the breast beneath. It takes about two-and-a-half years for the breasts to become fully formed. Throughout this time hormone activity increases the production of fluid from the vagina, but it is usually more than two years after the appearance of a breast bud that the menarche occurs.

Depending on a girl's preparation for this event, she is usually pleased, sometimes shocked, and occasionally afraid. Some girls whose mothers had told them about menstrual periods say that menarche still came as a shock. For some reason — perhaps a sense of guilt engendered by their mothers during childhood — they have "wiped out" the information.

Menarche does not coincide with the first ovulation (it has been known for a girl to become pregnant before menarche). Regular ovulation usually begins a year later, and may be signaled by a regularity of periods and premenstrual signs such as tenderness of the breasts or period pains in the abdomen. Axillary hair (in the armpits) begins also to grow at about this time. By the age of fourteen, most girls have developed all of these secondary sexual characteristics.

Puberty usually begins for a boy between the ages of thirteen and fifteen-and-a-half. At first the skin of the scrotum changes color, enlarges a little and alters texture; these changes are accompanied by an increase in the size of the testes. It is not uncommon for boys to develop a small mass of enlarged breast tissue beneath the nipples during this time. This may leave them open to teasing in the dressing room, but the condition usually resolves within three to thirteen months. Occasionally the enlargement is so noticeable that corrective surgery is advised.

The penis soon begins to enlarge and a small quantity of straight and unpigmented hair grows at its base. Over the next year the penis continues to enlarge, mostly in length, the scrotum and testes grow, and the pubic hair becomes more abundant, darker and curled. As the average boy reaches his

In boys, as in girls, the onset of puberty is controlled by hormones secreted from the pituitary gland. In boys the hormone responsible for secondary sexual characteristics is produced by the testes. This hormone — testosterone — affects sperm production and the development of the genitalia. The hypothalamus reacts to the blood level of this hormone and adjusts its release by the pituitary.

fifteenth year the penis thickens and the glans (tip) becomes enlarged, assuming an adult shape.

The time at which a boy's voice deepens (breaks), because of the alteration in the tension of the vocal chords, varies between individuals. A boy may not produce substantial facial hair until his twenties, although most young men begin to shave in their late teens. Chest hair, if present, continues to thicken late into the twenties.

The Adolescent Growth Spurt

Adolescence is the final phase of change, and the development of sexual characteristics coincides with the last period of rapid growth. This may appear much more significant than even the rate of growth of a baby during the first year, because the child has grown so steadily throughout childhood. During adolescence a boy grows on average eight inches taller, and during one year alone may grow a full four inches in height. For girls the growth spurt is less dramatic — the peak height gain is three and a quarter inches in a year, and after this growth continues at a much slower rate. Girls have usually finished growing by the age of eighteen, but for boys there may well be at least another inch of growing to come. A young man may not stop growing completely until he reaches the age of twenty-one.

Usually the hands and feet grow first, then the arms and legs begin to lengthen, then the shoulders become broader, and finally the trunk of the body grows. But these are not the only changes that occur to the skeleton. Some of the greatest alterations are to the skull itself, particularly the bones of the upper and lower jaw. As a result, the face — particularly of a boy — can change appearance quite considerably over a period of only a few months.

The muscular system has to keep pace with the skeletal system. Because girls start adolescence earlier than boys, most of the females in a school year are stronger and taller than the boys of the same age for about twelve months. Research has shown that in a girl the increased strength is caused by an increase in the size of the fibers within the muscles, but a boy may actually increase the number as well as the size of fibers. Boys, particularly, develop muscle across the shoulders

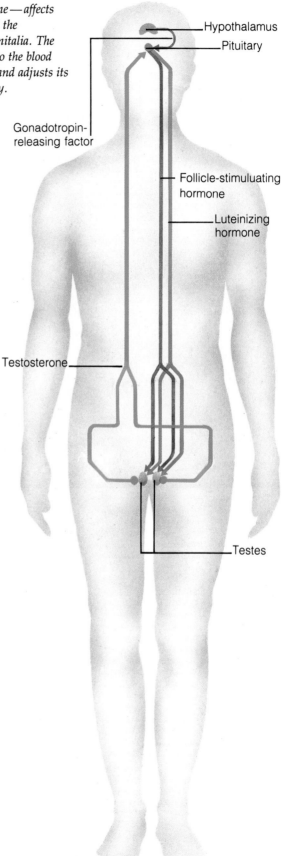

Hypothalamus

Pituitary

Gonadotropin-releasing factor

Follicle-stimuluating hormone

Luteinizing hormone

Testosterone

Testes

It is not until puberty that boys have the ability to build up muscle through weight training or other athletic activity, because this depends on the presence in the body of the hormone testosterone.

and in the back, but a girl's muscle development is more uniform. The lack of the male hormone testosterone in mature women means that, unlike men, they cannot produce such dramatic muscling through training.

Other organs rapidly increase in size during this time. The kidneys, spleen and liver grow, as does the heart — the latter has the capacity to increase up to fifty per cent in volume under training between the ages of twelve and sixteen, although for most adolescents the increase is not as much as this. The only system that does not grow is the lymphatic system (parts of which actually decrease in size).

The growth spurt is usually preceded by the laying down of fat in both boys and girls. Most boys around the age of twelve go through a period of chubbiness, but this soon disappears when height begins to increase rapidly. After the growth spurt fat is again laid down, although a young adult does not assume the tubby shape of the twelve-year-old, because the fat is distributed around the body in a different way.

For girls the laying down of fat is not completely altered by the ensuing growth spurt. A girl accumulates subcutaneous fat for about a year before the growth spurt, but thereafter retains more subcutaneous fat than a boy and it is distributed generally as well as in particular areas, giving her the characteristic figure of an adult woman.

Eating patterns change dramatically during this time, mostly because of the sudden growth but also because of the adolescent's changing emotions and desires. A recent survey showed that on average teenagers eat more than three times a day; that they snack more and eat full meals less; that breakfast is the most often missed meal, girls missing it more often than boys; that snacks are high in sugar; and that protein intake is less in girls than boys.

These findings show that the adolescent has a high chance of not eating the diet needed by the rapidly growing body. Energy requirements can be satisfied by sugary or carbohydrate-rich snacks, but the intake of protein and necessary minerals and vitamins can suffer. Adolescents need encouragement and guidance. Moral ideals may also be important to them — many become vegetarians.

At the peak of the growth spurt boys need as many Calories as does an adult man doing a manual job, about 3,300 Calories per day: girls need about 2,500 Calories, rather more than an average adult woman. Girls face more critical choices about nutrition than do boys during this time. Their need for a high calorie intake falls off sharply at the end of the growth spurt, and many are more subject to body-orientated pressures to maintain a "perfect" figure than are boys.

One of the results of the diet followed to a greater or lesser extent by most adolescents is that oral hygiene may be at risk. The situation is worsened by the fact that visits to the dentist are much less in the hands of the parents and clashes can occur within the family if the subject of oral care is mishandled. A sympathetic dentist is the key person in this situation. If he or she makes the adolescent feel like a proper person, the patient will participate willingly in the treatment.

Psychosexuality and Rebellion

In addition to all the physical changes that take place during puberty, an adolescent has to mature

psychologically and this often gives rise to behavioral problems. It is difficult to discuss the problems of the adolescent without basing them on sexuality, because the basic difference between a child and an adult is that an adult can reproduce. However, some parents tend to dwell on minor irritations, such as the teenager's need to conform to the peer group in modes of dress or styles of hair, when the essence of the problem lies in the teenager's quest to find his or her true self. These emotions are biologically strong—throughout the history of evolution, successful reproduction is the key to a successful species.

Sexuality is not exclusively adult, it emerges gradually throughout babyhood and childhood, but with the onset of puberty sexual interest increases rapidly.

Between the ages of twelve and fourteen, most boys experiment with autostimulation (masturbation), and according to the foundations laid by earlier experiences within the family, they either feel guilty about it or not. Some boys unnecessarily fear that masturbation and night emissions may use up their quota of sperm, making them infertile as adults, but a boy who has discussed both topics with the well-informed family generally has no problems adjusting.

Often such experimentation begins after discussion and demonstration within a group of friends (peer group), and this illustrates the changing principle behind the acquisition of knowledge about sex. Until puberty it is a gradual process deriving from the family itself; after puberty most teenagers are less able to accept this type of knowledge from adults, and subsequent learning tends to come from within the peer group. Boorish behavior toward women may be a blind to disguise a boy's intense interest in the opposite sex.

In adolescence, many boys are given more freedom by their parents than are girls of the same

Sexual awareness is heightened in adolescence and many teenagers read erotic literature as a form of sexual learning. Such erotica tend, however, to portray a misguided image of the average human body, which is rarely of model proportions and appearance. It also suggests that people are always ready and available for sex — a view guaranteed to disappoint and one which is potentially harmful.

age. Boys' relationships with their mothers may settle down quickly, or not, according to the personalities involved, but often mothers continue to "spoil" their adolescent sons by treating them as though they are still helpless children.

Boys have strong peer groups within which they may discuss various aspects of sex, which helps to make them feel that the difficulties they face are common to everyone and so they can accept the changes of their bodies more readily.

Girls frequently have problems adjusting to their growing sexuality. They may want to be attractive to men but at the same time be afraid that this is a goal they will never achieve, and so hide behind a "tomboy" image. Rebellion in young adolescent girls is common, and parents — fearing the possible consequences of such strong emotions — may easily overreact and restrict their daughters too much.

For both boys and girls actual sexual activities are still comparatively rare within this early age group.

Experimentation tends to be at a lower intensity, usually as part of a group, and couples usually have a purely physical interest in one another. Among a mixed group of fifteen-year-olds, the boys tend to relate to one another, whereas the girls tend to relate to members of the opposite sex in a slightly more senior age group.

Mid and Late Adolescence

Early adolescence is usually complete for girls by the age of fifteen, and about a year later for boys. The growth spurt has slowed down and the main secondary sexual characteristics are well established. This can be a time when emotional turmoils within the teenager become reduced, but if conflicts have been allowed to reach a severe state during early adolescence, a teenager may even decide to break away altogether, and run away from home.

Teenagers of both sexes are excessively concerned about their body image, and comparisons

Stress due to the dramatic physical and emotional changes of puberty can be great, and is often characterized by some degree of temporary psychological disturbance (below), such as depression, or *irrationally dramatic acts such as running away from home. A growing awareness of sexually defined gender roles is also an important feature of puberty, although traditional* characterizations are changing. For instance, Tom Sawyer would have been horrified to see a girl fishing (below right), *but since the time Mark Twain was writing such distinctions have diminished.*

within the peer group are the subject of much discussion. Posture problems often begin during adolescence — girls unable to accept having large breasts may adopt a habitual roundness to the shoulders and take to wearing loose-fitting clothing; similarly an excessively tall boy may stoop to lessen his height.

The older adolescent does, however, have the ability to think abstractly; he or she can work out the consequences of certain actions and make quantitative judgments. The teenager may become highly creative and channel thoughts into poetry, writing, drama, art or music. Gradually an interest in adult behavior becomes prominent. The teenager wants to succeed in the adult world, and generally leaves behind the same-sex interests of the peer group to build truly heterosexual relationships. The teenager who is given more freedom from home at this stage may feel less anxious about the need to leave home. Over-restricted girls particularly tend to marry early or take jobs, skipping further

education to break away from home. Boys tend to feel more comfortable in the home for longer. Although few teenagers actively want parental control, most still need and usually respect genuine advice, praise and approval.

Research suggests that the average age at which a girl has her first full sexual experience is eighteen; for boys it is usually later. This is explained not only by the fact that girls mature earlier, but also by the different fulfillments they seek. Girls tend to be more concerned with finding and maintaining loving relationships; many boys regard sexual experience as a learning and proving ground. These different attitudes are reflected in the large numbers of girls at this age who regard themselves as "engaged."

Sexually-transmitted diseases and unwanted pregnancies are by no means confined to adolescents, yet they should have access to sound information on these subjects. Wild stories and exaggerations are rife within peer groups, so that it

is advisable for parents to make certain that their teenage children have correct knowledge.

Problems for Adolescents

Because body-image is so important to a teenager, many of the physical changes seem to be ironically cruel at a time when a person has a need to look perfect. For a boy, the sudden activity in the apocrine glands causes increased sweating and body odor; for a girl her menstrual cycle produces recurring rashes of spots. Hormonal changes increase the amount of sebum from glands in the skin, particularly in the scalp and around the face; seborrheic dermatitis associated with this increased activity causes dandruff.

The most upsetting of these types of disorders is acne vulgaris. The primary lesion is a comedo (blackhead), a collection of oxidized sebum plugging a hair follicle. Blackheads are common on the face and neck as well as the chest and back, and from these acne develops in the form of inflamed, red pustules. Occasionally they can turn into cysts. Early treatment of acne often prevents it from becoming disfiguring, but a teenager has to

appreciate that treatment may take a few months to show an improvement.

It is now thought that diet does not have a particularly profound effect on the severity of acne, although ultraviolet rays in sunlight certainly have a beneficial effect; during winter ultraviolet therapy may be used. If the face is left scarred, dermabrasion (the surgical removal of the top layer of skin) can be carried out in adulthood by a dermatologist or plastic surgeon.

Most adolescent girls are worried about their figures; many experiment with "fad" diets. Some swing too far beyond normal behavior and become so obsessed with weight loss that they develop a potentially lethal condition known as anorexia nervosa. The condition is much less common among males, although some experts now recognize excessive long-distance running as a similar type of retreat in adult men.

The causes of anorexia are not fully understood but by excessive dieting a girl can delay her adolescence, she can stop menstruating, and delay breast development and the forming of an adult female shape. Anorectics may also suffer from guilt

complexes and many of them have unusually dominant mothers.

The anorectic has a misguided body-image, and even when she is skeletally thin, the girl may still maintain that she is fat. In some forms of anorexia the girl gorges on a variety of extraordinary foods then vomits; in others excessive use may be made of laxatives. Like an alcoholic, the anorectic is subtle and cunning at hiding her problem but soon external signs make it obvious — the skin changes and becomes scaly, and the girl usually becomes severely depressed.

Early treatment is the key to a cure. Once the girl is more than twenty-five pounds under the average weight for her age and height the condition becomes more difficult to treat, and five per cent of anorectics die. For those who are apparently cured, usually by hospitalization and psychotherapy within the family, as many as sixty per cent undergo a relapse. Anorexia in adolescence usually persists, if only in a mild form, well into adulthood. The opposite problem, bulimia, is overeating because of an abnormal increase in hunger. It affects ten per cent of American college girls.

Anorexia is rare in males, whose problems may be more physical. For instance, an adolescent boy who has not been circumcised may experience problems if the foreskin is tight; such phimosis becomes apparent when erections become more frequent. If the foreskin becomes lodged behind the enlarged head of the penis, causing acute pain, an emergency circumcision is usually required. If pain is felt during erection, the teenager may be advised to have an elective circumcision, which is a relatively minor operation.

Alcohol, Smoking and Drugs

Teenagers like to experiment. They cannot avoid coming into contact with drinkers and smokers, and many also come into contact with users of drugs. This usually happens when they are away from parental control, so what can a family do to prevent addiction? An obvious answer is to make sure that young people are fully informed about the dangers of drinking, smoking and drug abuse. But who should convey this information to them? And in what form?

Experts have studied patterns within groups of teenagers. In order of importance, the influences on them are: the peer group, the desire to be part of an older group, parental attitude, and attitude to health. The first two categories are hard to control — nearly all teenagers resent any interference from parents into their peer groups — but the third and fourth points can be influenced by the stance adopted by the parents.

As far as alcohol is concerned, figures show that teenagers from homes where alcohol is consumed in moderate quantities and who learn to drink at home, usually avoid alcohol abuse later. They learn a respect for alcohol and can test their limits of tolerance in the safety of the family circle, as long as parents take a fairly relaxed and humorous attitude toward overindulgence. Hopefully by the time they are in the potentially lethal situation of deciding whether to drink and drive a car, they have developed a more realistic attitude toward their limitations.

Cigarette smoking must be handled in exactly the opposite way. Most teenagers are quick to kick against double standards within a family, and if the parents are smokers their children are far more likely to start themselves. Of the teenagers who smoke before the age of twenty, eighty-five per cent do not give up in later life. If they do not smoke before the age of twenty, they are unlikely ever to do so.

Thinking parents make sure that teenagers understand parental attitudes toward smoking and the risks that smoking involves, even though teenagers tend to feel invincible and have difficulty envisaging a healthless future for themselves. Parents are within their rights to ban smoking in the home — this may not stop a teenager from smoking at all but it will cut down on cigarette consumption.

Many teenagers encounter abuse of drugs such as cannabis and, increasingly, cocaine. Again, parents should be certain that teenagers understand the dangers of drugs — much of this can be discussed during late childhood when the opinions of parents carry more weight. Some counselors believe that it is unwise for parents to come down too hard on the use of cannabis, because this may undermine their arguments on the subject of hard

Many adolescents like to experiment as part of their growing need for independence, but too often they do not appreciate the risks. These are significant for health in the case of smoking, but can be deadly where drugs like heroin are concerned. This poster (bottom) is part of the British government's attempt to discourage people from experimenting with heroin by illustrating the results of its use.

drugs. Others believe that any form of drug-taking should be consistently condemned.

The Final Break

Adolescence is a time of discovery, experimentation and change. An adolescent may be moody and rebellious, but he or she is usually also vital, energetic and inspired. Many of the patterns of living that emerge during adolescence benefit not only the individual but also their own children in years to come. For families guiding a son or daughter through this bumpy phase of life, some form of relationship — however tenuous — needs to be maintained, because it is on this that child and parent can rebuild as the offspring enters adulthood. Teenagers may deliberately "experiment" with extreme forms of behavior or dress, sometimes merely to test parental reaction. Parents owe it to their children to make them feel confident in themselves. With confidence comes the ability to use the moral attitudes that the parents have grounded them in through childhood, because it is according to these that the teenager must decide between personal desire and personal restriction.

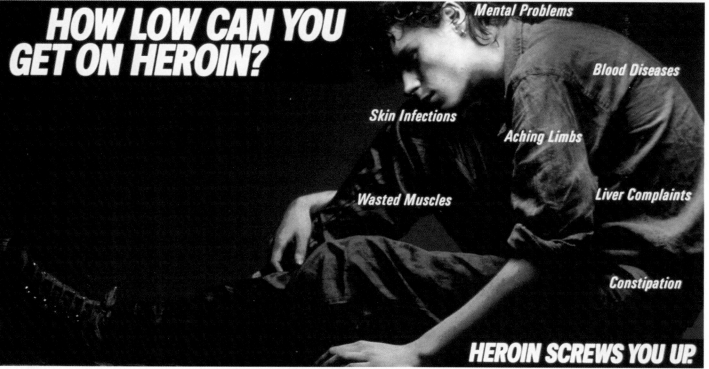

HOW LOW CAN YOU GET ON HEROIN?

Mental Problems

Blood Diseases

Skin Infections

Aching Limbs

Wasted Muscles

Liver Complaints

Constipation

HEROIN SCREWS YOU UP.

Chapter 6

The Road to Maturity

Aging can be said to begin in the womb, for even the earliest embryonic cells divide, multiply, serve out their time and die. By the time physical growth ceases, the process of aging is well underway. But unlike the growth of children it is by no means an even process, punctuated by clear-cut milestones. In fact people differ so much in the manner and extent of their aging that the boundaries become less distinct as time goes by. Some people seem to be born "middle-aged" in their attitudes; some appear old at fifty; others remain sprightly well into their eighties and nineties.

But at the dawn of adulthood, the young person is reaching his or her physical peak. Growth is virtually complete; organs reach their maximum weight in the early twenties and will not begin a gradual shrinkage for another two decades. Muscle power is well developed, although, depending on life style, it has potential for further development to peak at the age of thirty, declining by about ten per cent over the next three decades. Reaction time, which has been sharpening throughout childhood and adolescence, reaches a plateau by about the twentieth year and starts to tail off imperceptibly by the twenty-sixth.

The aging process is already at work — loss of hearing, for instance, begins in adolescence — but who in their twenties wants to know? The decline is barely perceptible, and in any case, most fit, active young people are rarely preoccupied with the state of the organism. The concern is with careers, money, relationships and leisure pursuits, for it is in these years of peak physical viability that the foundations are laid for the whole of the remaining adult span.

What Causes Aging?

Some gerontologists believe that aging is a "whole body" process, probably resulting from the activities of hormones and the organs and functions they control. Maintenance systems such as the

In defiance of their advancing years, high-spirited senior citizens participate whole-heartedly in a game of snowballs — an activity usually reserved for children. Despite a certain amount of physical impairment accompanying old age, most people can now be expected to live healthy, happy and fulfilling lives well beyond retirement.

Continuous exposure to harsh environmental conditions may hasten the aging process in certain parts of the body. Most at risk are unprotected regions such as the face, eyes and hands.

immune system may fail or glandular activity, such as that of the thyroid, may be interrupted. It has even been postulated that there might exist an "aging hormone" (just as there is, for example, a growth hormone), but so far no such substance has been found.

Other scientists attribute the aging of an individual to the aging of the cells of which he or she is composed. Even in the womb before birth, some fetal cells "wear out" and die, to be replaced by new ones. Alongside the cell multiplication that is essential for growth and development to take place, cell death and replacement continues. But there appears to be a finite limit to the number of times cells can renew themselves — about fifty times according to the observations of the American cell biologist Leonard Hayflick. In patients with the rare disorder progeria or Werner's syndrome (characterized by premature aging), however, the number of potential cell doublings falls far short of the normal fifty or so.

If aging is dependent on cellular processes, then the controller of the cells — the DNA in their nuclei — may somehow be ultimately responsible. This, in turn, suggests a possible genetic component in aging; certainly longevity seems to run in some families. Based on experiments with animals, other researchers postulate that highly active chemicals known as free radicals can damage DNA and disrupt the cellular control process. If this is so, it is theoretically possible that antioxidants could be used to "mop up" free radicals and prevent their disruptive action; in other words, they might slow down aging.

Early Adulthood

Physically, people in their twenties and thirties are at their best. There are hardly any age-specific disorders that affect them — one of the chief causes of hospitalization in young adults, particularly men, is accidents. Most people contract minor ailments, such as the common cold or influenza, and allergies and migraine headaches continue to plague those who are susceptible to them. But on the whole early adulthood is a time of physical fitness.

Good health tends to center on life style. It does not necessarily occur to people at this stage that the foundations of a rigorous old age are laid in youth: a person who adopts a healthy life style in the early years makes a positive investment toward good health in old age. It is, after all, well recognized that bad habits early on — such as lack of exercise, poor diet, smoking and excessive drinking — may be more of a factor in producing some of the problems common in later life, including cardio-vascular disease, cancer and diabetes, than the aging process itself.

In terms of life choices, the possibilities may sometimes seem baffling to a young adult. With changing social conditions, many more careers are open to all-comers — although, with the experience of world recession still smarting, the competition for jobs is perhaps stiffer than ever. Except in local areas of real deprivation, where unemployment is high and jobs once secured must be kept at all costs, there is more movement across the employment spectrum today than there has been at any time in the past.

Life styles are changing, too. The conventional idyll of meeting a partner, marrying and having two or three children is no longer sacrosanct. Many people now choose to marry late or indeed to remain single. In 1960 some six million single Americans in their thirties said they had no intention of marrying, and the number of singles is known to have increased since then. In 1976, the United States Government Bureau of the Census noted, in its publication *Household and Family Characteristics*, that of nine and a half million new households reported during the previous five years, seventy per cent consisted of people living alone, or with others unrelated by marriage, or of women running households without the support of a man.

Census officials also reported that, by 1976, 52.1 per cent of American households comprised only one or two people (compared with 40.9 per cent in 1960). This means that two-parent families with children are a minority. In the United States,

as in Western society generally, more and more couples are choosing not to have children or to limit themselves to one or two. The reasons for this drop in the birthrate are complex, but financial pressures, career commitments and a spiraling divorce rate — nearly half of all American marriages are formally "put asunder" — are clearly important contributing factors.

The period from thirty to forty-five years of age is mostly one of consolidation in all departments: career, marriage (with or without children) or alternative partnership, friendships and social pursuits. Although the process of aging is running its inexorable course, the cumulative effects are negligible. This is a productive time when, although some people view the approach of their fortieth birthday as a tragedy of cosmic proportions, old age still seems relatively distant. Professional and social recognition begin to accrue; experience is mounting; financial pressures should begin to ease.

But, against this ideal, it is salutary to reflect that life experience is not the same for all. In poorer nations of the world, a man or woman can be old at forty. Even in the West, manual workers have been found to consider themselves middle-aged at thirty-five, whereas white-collar personnel push this particular hurdle back to at least fifty. In this age group, men generally mark the passing of time by career events, including increments in pay; women (other than those wholly wedded to their careers) tend to mark off the years by the growth and development of their children.

The Onset of Middle Age

The infamous "mid-life crisis" — if and when it comes — reflects these preoccupations. But it is also to do with altered physical appearance, health worries, changing levels of sexual activity, and not altogether morbid fears about advancing age. Some women may experience the so-called "empty nest syndrome" watching their children leave home, others welcome the chance of renewed career involvement or the luxury of doing as they please, free of day-to-day household demands. In many ways there are parallels here with the adolescent identity crisis and, as in their teens, some people in mid-life may make sudden and sometimes ap-

During the 1960s and 1970s, communal living was popular with many American young people. Youthful experiments with alternative ways of life are usually abandoned before middle age.

parently irrational changes in their circumstances — walking out on their partners, perhaps, or throwing over an executive life style to scratch a living from the land.

For women there is the very definite marker of the menopause, which normally occurs between the ages of forty-five and fifty-five. The menopause — probably the most scrutinized age-linked change in all human biology — signifies the end of reproductive capacity. Menstruation ceases, ovulation no longer takes place and there is no futher hormonal input to maintain fertility. These endocrine changes — specifically the suppression of estrogen — are responsible for well-known post-menopausal symptoms such as atrophy of the breasts and genital tissues, hot flashes and accelerated weakening of the bones (osteoporosis). However, hormone replacement therapy (HRT), still widely practiced, is now administered with precautions appropriate to counter the established connection between the administration of estrogen and uterine cancer.

For years, people have talked of the possibility of a male climacteric, akin to the female menopause. But in reality there is no such phenomenon. Men experience no sharp endocrine changes, although testosterone levels decrease gradually with age. Sperm counts are reduced in the later years, but men normally remain fertile and capable of fathering children throughout life.

The main problem with sex in later life is not so much a physical one as the shadow cast by misinformed beliefs — the outdated view, for instance, that sex in the later years is somehow not nice, or that older people are "past it." True, there is some falling off in libido — less with those who remain fairly active — but men do not normally or automatically become impotent at fifty nor women lose interest after the menopause.

Many women, however, free at last of the fear of

117

The successful businesswoman overturns many traditional attitudes, not only toward criteria of achievement, but also toward family and home. Such a woman may try to combine her career with a full domestic life, although this can lead to unexpected areas of physical and mental stress, particularly if children are too demanding or if her partner is unwilling to accept her unconventional role.

pregnancy, find more — rather than less — enjoyment in sex in the post-menopausal years. As Kinsey, Masters and Johnson, and others have repeatedly shown, sexual capacity is lifelong and many people continue to exercise it well into old age. The important point to remember is that there really is no difference in sex before or after fifty. If the whole thing was unsatisfactory in the earlier years it is unlikely to improve at that point.

Between the ages of forty-five and sixty meanwhile, ill health becomes more common, and the death rate during this period is double that of the preceding years. The principal causes of death in middle age — and indeed in later life — are heart disease, cancer, circulatory disorders, stroke and diseases of the respiratory system.

Working and Retiring

Meanwhile, given good health and marginal decline still in the later middle years, the next great landmark to be passed is retirement — welcomed by some, anathema to others. Although in many ways controversial, the trend toward younger retirement brings in people in the prime of life to provide a strong and vigorous baseline to the retired population as a whole. Yet many people do not want to retire. About one-third of retired Americans would like to be working, at least part-time, and no less than three-quarters of those still in employment would like to go on to some kind of paid, part-time work.

In Japan the urge to work is stronger still. Although the rate of employment among the elderly has been dropping steadily (thirty years ago it was 42 per cent), 26.3 per cent of Japanese are still working beyond the age of sixty-five, compared with 12.3 per cent in the United States. Far from sitting back to cultivate their *bonsai*, more Japanese would continue to work if they could; a survey revealed that the number of elderly jobless actively

A diet high in cholesterol will, over a period of years, cause the walls of a healthy artery (below) to become clogged with fatty deposits which eventually enlarge and thicken (right). When this happens, it causes a reduction in blood flow through the artery. This condition, commonly known as "hardening of the arteries" (atherosclerosis), is the chief cause of heart attacks, and may be responsible for strokes.

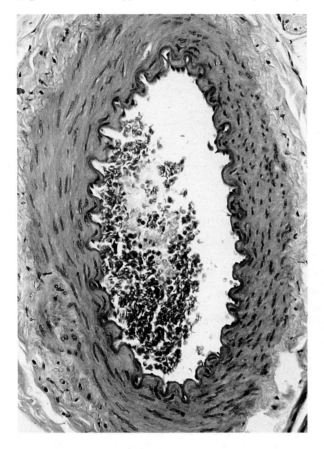
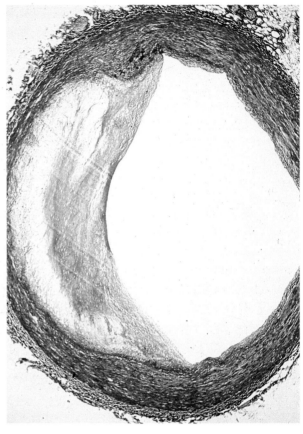

seeking employment had doubled in a recent ten-year period.

The British veteran campaigner Alex Comfort recalls the much-quoted galaxy of golden oldies — peopled by creative folk in particular — who have achieved and created and performed and generally captured the headlines at a very advanced age. In his book *A Good Age*, he says: "Two weeks is about the ideal length of time to retire."

For most people, however, the key to successful retirement is facing up to it — and well ahead of time. This is the message of many organizations set up to help employees nearing retirement. The American Association of Retired Persons (AARP) claims to be the largest organization of its kind, with a membership of more than seven million. Early on the AARP found that many of the problems of retirement would never have arisen with proper foresight and planning. So it developed an offshoot called AIM (Action for

Independent Maturity) to cater for those coming up to retirement.

There is no magic formula for structuring a happy and constructive old age, but there are a few practical and philosophical arrangements that can help. It is a question of putting affairs in order and priming the morale for the transition that comes with advancing age. In an ideal world, perhaps, the human life span would be seen as a continuum, offering new challenges and opportunities along its length. This way, people could continue developing their potentials and put their skills to work throughout life — irrespective of calendar age.

Today, it is hard to know where old age begins, and accordingly it is true to say that Western society in general is becoming top-heavy with senior citizens. This "graying of nations" — what one leading British geriatrician has called the "survival of the unfittest" — is evident not least in the United States, where average life expectancy has increased by more than twenty-five years during the course of this century (from forty-seven years in 1900 to seventy-three years in 1980). Already estimated at eleven per cent, the elderly population is expected to double in the next half century (whereas total US population growth is projected at only forty per cent). The number of very old people will rise even faster: the over-seventy-fives will form from thirty-five to forty-five per cent of the US elderly population and the number of over-eighty-fives will treble, from the present two million to six million, within the next fifty years.

What this demographic shift means is that more people than ever are living out a normal life span. What it has mainly provoked, apart from token rumbles of concern, is a renewed interest in the relatively new discipline of gerontology.

The first message that gerontologists are keen to have understood is that old age is not in itself a disease. Sick old people are sick because they are sick, not because they are old. With adequate care and provision, these later years can be used to develop what Dr Comfort describes as a useful and productive "second trajectory" — a time which brings joy and fulfillment rather than the burdens hitherto associated with old age.

The Aging Body

The causes of aging are unknown. Some theories center round the fact that cells are not immortal. In the laboratory they are seen to have a finite life, which is shorter with advancing donor age. Interestingly, too, cells from people with diseases characterized by premature aging, such as Werner's syndrome or progeria, do not survive as long in culture as those from fit people matched for age. There is the theory, alternatively, that some process of chemical assault attacks both the body's cellular and inert tissues. This has led to experiments with chemicals known as antioxidants to slow aging, and these do indeed make laboratory mice live longer. But they also upset their metabolism, and it could be that any gain in life span results simply from the fact that the mice eat less.

It is, however, agreed that each species has a maximum characteristic life span; it is around one hundred and ten years in the case of human beings.

A period of rehabilitation may be necessary for elderly people who have broken bones in a fall. Brittle bones and slower reflexes all contribute to making falls the most common type of accident in the elderly.

Reports of preposterously long-lived peasants in some mountainous communities where centenarians are a dime a dozen — in the Caucasus, for instance, and the Andes — are probably evidence more of local whimsy and the absence of reliable birth records than of truly exceptional longevity.

Although it is probably futile to look for an extended life span, it is possible to contemplate increasing average life expectancy (which has already gone from less than twenty years in ancient Greece to more than seventy years in the United States today). But the gains still to be made are small. If heart disease — which is the leading cause of death in the United States — were eliminated, life expectancy at birth would increase by only seven years; the conquest of cancer would give an extra three years. In fact, if the ten foremost killer complaints were all knocked out, the bonus in life expectancy would be little more than a decade. Having dodged disease, people would eventually still die of old age — in the real world there is no Shangri-la.

The rate of aging does not increase as life goes by; for the most part a thirty-year-old is aging just as fast as an octogenarian. True, older people have undergone more changes simply because they have lived longer, but they are not losing function any faster than younger people. There is some variability from person to person, from organ to organ, from function to function. Some activities — such as the output of the heart, the filtration rate of the kidneys and the ability to metabolize carbohydrates — tend to alter quite dramatically. But others — the speed of nerve conduction or the manufacture of red blood cells — show no significant changes well into old age. There is, however, no respite from aging, no plateau in life where people remain at peak functioning for a couple of decades.

The changes are gradual ones; for example, the skin does not suddenly wrinkle or the hair change color overnight. But over the years the skin loses elasticity and some of the subcutaneous fat disappears, causing sagging and wrinkling. There is a change in pigmentation — mainly a reduction in melanocytes — and the hair loses color. These changes in the skin (which becomes very fragile with great age) are most marked in the exposed parts of the body. There is some loss of muscle mass

As a person gets older, wear and tear on the larger weight-bearing joints, such as the hips, knees or spine, may cause the condition known as osteoarthritis. Joints that have been badly crippled by osteoarthritis (below left) *can be replaced with artificial ones. These are usually made of metal or a combination of metal and plastic. If the replacement is successful it helps improve movement and relieve pain and,* more importantly for many elderly people, restores a large measure of independence and of the quality of life. The most common replacements are those of hip joints (below right and bottom).

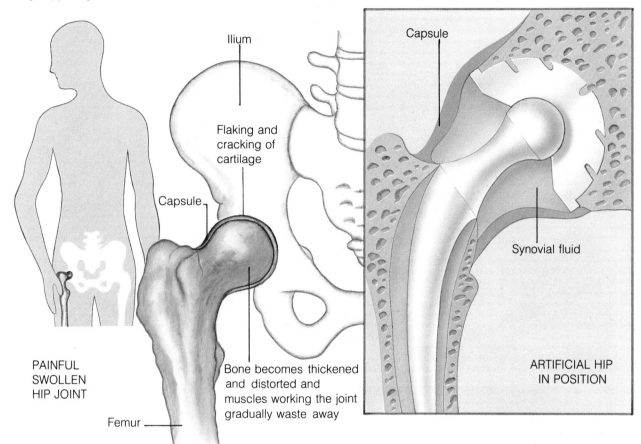

Ilium

Capsule

Flaking and cracking of cartilage

Capsule

PAINFUL SWOLLEN HIP JOINT

Bone becomes thickened and distorted and muscles working the joint gradually waste away

Femur

Synovial fluid

ARTIFICIAL HIP IN POSITION

as muscle itself is replaced by fibrous tissue. Muscle atrophy is hastened by disuse, which is one of the many good reasons for continued activity. The capacity for moderate physical endeavor does not decline with age, although the limit for hard work is lowered.

Changes in bones and joints can be more troublesome. From the thirties onward there is progressive bone loss, which starts earlier in women and accelerates after the menopause. This overall, but not uniform, reduction in skeletal mass is thought to result from impaired calcium absorption and increased calcium loss in the urine; where it becomes pathological it is classified as metabolic bone disease. Bones become brittle and are more liable to fracture. Cartilage thickens and there is increased calcification of joint structures, with loss of elasticity and stiffening. Old people lose height because of the shrinking of the disks between the vertebrae and a tendency to stoop.

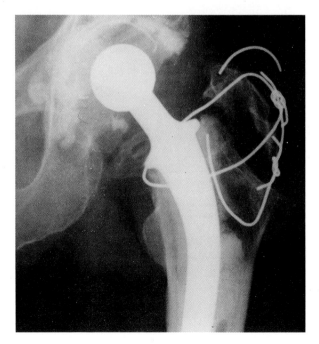

Most people are capable of working efficiently beyond the mandatory retirement age (below). However, it is sometimes necessary for elderly people to turn to alternative tasks that they can accomplish satisfactorily despite the decline in their physical abilities. Many industrial operations (bottom) are carried out at a reasonable pace, and are well within the working capacity of older operatives.

Within the body cavities, organs and systems undergo a loss of efficiency. The heart itself tends to hypertrophy under the burden of time and its output is reduced (although it may still increase sevenfold under stress); the aorta, the body's great arterial highway, dilates with age; arterial pathways narrow, becoming furred with plaque through the inevitable presence of cholesterol; many byways in the distant capillary network shut down altogether. Blood pressure tends to rise with advancing age — more so in Westernized society than in less developed countries, which suggests some genetic or environmental factor rather than mere aging as such.

Peak lung function is reached in the early twenties and falls off gradually with age because of decreasing efficiency in the actual mechanics of breathing as well as the growing inelasticity of tissues within the lung. The result is that progressively less oxygen is available for uptake by the blood. Good ventilation depends on physical movement: prolonged sitting or bed rest are hazardous for elderly lungs.

The aging gut is less ready to process vast

Since 1900 in the United States, average life expectancy at birth has risen from 47 to 69 years for males, and from 51 to 75 years for females. The graph shows the death rate of the population as a percentage by age.

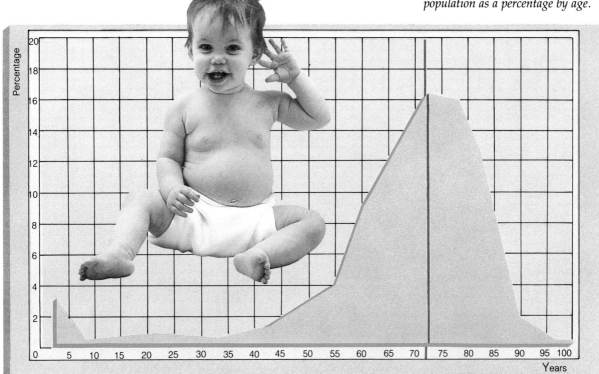

quantities of food. Secretion of saliva and gastric juices is reduced; gastric motility decreases slightly; the gut itself shrinks. But the absorption of nutrients, with the exception of fats and calcium, is not usually impaired. There are, however, changes in the liver which have important consequences for the metabolism of some drugs and foods. Although this massive organ does not diminish in size, its blood-flow is cut back by half from maturity to advanced old age.

Two of the main problems related to nutrition in old age are those of extremes: obesity and malnutrition. Obesity results from overeating and may be caused by a combination of boredom and reduced activity. It is usually an ongoing problem, however; most obese elders were obese as younger adults. The estimate of one gerontologist is that almost one-third of Americans die, either directly or indirectly, from overeating. Some people, however, drift in the other direction, gradually reaching a state of chronic malnourishment which may, in turn, lead to outright deficiency disorders.

Alterations in endocrine and metabolic systems with advancing age are of particular interest to gerontologists, because there is a question that the aging process itself may be secondary to endocrine changes. This possibility is underlined by the similarities between some states of hormone deficiency, such as myxedema and diabetes, and the effects of normal aging. In this area, impaired carbohydrate metabolism is one of the principal findings. Carbohydrate intolerance may mimic diabetes or indeed lead to the late-onset version of the disease itself, which is thought in any case to be present, if undetected, in at least one-quarter of the over-eighty-fives.

The kidneys, which lose almost one-third of their mass between young adulthood and the eighth decade, become less efficient at filtering off wastes from the blood. The actual filtration surface within the kidneys is reduced, and so is the renal blood supply. Salt and water balance is compromised, and a potentially serious effect (given that there is a decrease in total body water with age) is that the elderly dehydrate faster than younger people. This is especially so in very hot weather, in the presence of fever, or if, as often happens, fluid intake is reduced to less than three to five pints a day.

Perhaps possessing the secret of longevity, centenarians such as the Russian Levan Sajaya celebrating his 115th birthday (below) *appear youthful and active, often without hint of disorder or disability that usually accompanies very old age. Most individuals who reach a great age remain at work. Charlie Chaplin* (right) *was still involved with motion pictures when he died in 1977 at the age of 87 years.*

Some sensory loss is to be expected, too. The two most common effects are a reduced ability of the eyes to focus on close objects — the well-known trouble with the small print — and a degree of hearing loss, particularly for the higher tones. Mechanisms of balance become less accurate; kinesthesia, the sense of movement and position, diminishes with age. Taste, smell and touch are reduced to some degree. The cumulative effects of sensory loss in the elderly are of obvious concern.

But, contrary to popular myth, the healthy brain does not atrophy or degenerate with age; it should function well throughout the normal span.

Illness and Old Age

In developed countries the old undergo fewer episodes of illness than younger people: an average of 1.3 per year, compared with 2.1 per person for all ages. Admittedly, 81 per cent of over-sixty-fives have some chronic health problem (as against only

54 per cent of younger people), but this may be something as easily managed as weak eyesight. It is the so-called "grand elderly" who may become a burden on the medical services, with the over-seventy-fives in the United States three to five times more likely to require assistance than those aged sixty-five to seventy-four. Still, less than five per cent of old people really require institutional care.

The main thrust of scientific gerontology is in distinguishing the changes brought about by the normal aging process from those caused by disease. Some diseases and disabilities, of course, are examples of accelerated aging. Osteoporosis is a progressive thinning of the bones which mostly afflicts women — there are fifteen million suf-ferers in the United States alone. But it is simply an exaggerated form of a process that occurs in everyone after the age of thirty-five. Osteoarthritis is an extreme manifestation of the normal wear and tear sustained by major joints. But in these conditions, where there are parallels with the normal aging process, there are clearly other factors at work: one arthritic hip is almost always worse than the other in the same person, although both are the same age.

Gerontologists have always insisted that a careful knowledge of normal aging is an essential prerequisite to the practice of geriatric medicine, in that if physicians are hazy about what is normal, they are much less likely to be sensitive to the abnormal. A classic example often quoted is that the elderly react quite differently to medication, not least because of the declining efficiency of the liver in which many drugs are metabolized. Frequently over-medicated, they are more inclined to suffer toxic effects.

Old people, too, exhibit symptoms different from those seen in younger patients with the same disease. In an elderly patient, the presenting symptom of acute pneumonia, for example, may be confusion, and this can be misinterpreted. In addition, there is a risk that symptoms may be attributed to normal aging and some reversible disorder go untreated. It is for these reasons that geriatric medicine has evolved as a separate clinical specialty, served by physicians with advanced knowledge of the aging human organism and the way in which it deteriorates.

Gray hair and wrinkles are two of the most unwelcome landmarks of aging. In some people, physical characteristics of aging appear relatively early in life, whereas in others they may hardly occur at all.

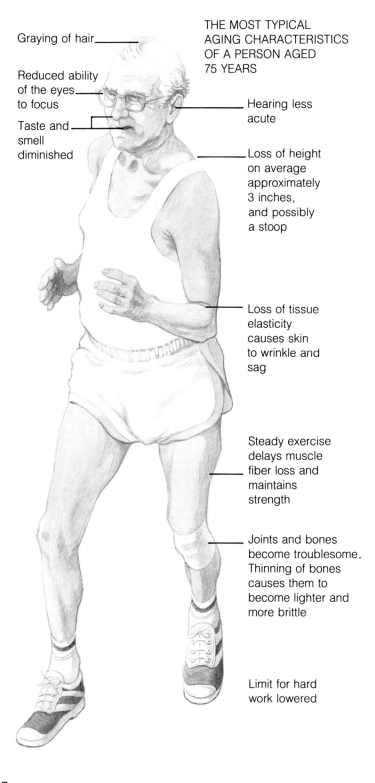

THE MOST TYPICAL AGING CHARACTERISTICS OF A PERSON AGED 75 YEARS

Graying of hair

Reduced ability of the eyes to focus

Taste and smell diminished

Hearing less acute

Loss of height on average approximately 3 inches, and possibly a stoop

Loss of tissue elasticity causes skin to wrinkle and sag

Steady exercise delays muscle fiber loss and maintains strength

Joints and bones become troublesome. Thinning of bones causes them to become lighter and more brittle

Limit for hard work lowered

The effect of age on different organs and bodily functions varies, but all become more susceptible to fatigue and disease. Organs such as the lungs and kidneys are less efficient at 60 than they were at 20 years old.

Young and old can often bridge the generation gap with great ease. Grandparents and granddaughter find no difficulty in communicating or in sharing interests and activities, such as a walk in the country.

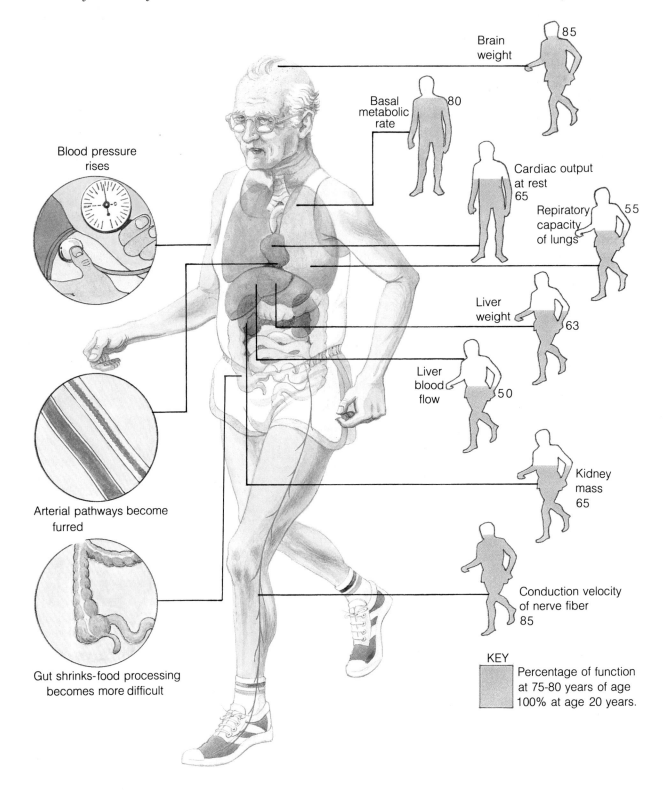

Brain weight 85

Basal metabolic rate 80

Blood pressure rises

Cardiac output at rest 65

Respiratory capacity of lungs 55

Liver weight 63

Liver blood flow 50

Arterial pathways become furred

Kidney mass 65

Conduction velocity of nerve fiber 85

Gut shrinks-food processing becomes more difficult

KEY
Percentage of function at 75-80 years of age 100% at age 20 years.

Clearly there are medical consequences of the aging process itself, especially within the cardio-vascular system. Arteries slowly harden with age and this deterioration is aggravated by atheroma, or arterial plaque, which furs up the inner walls of the blood vessels and by reducing flow may lead to strokes and heart disease. With their relatively inelastic lung tissue, the old are more at risk, too, from respiratory infections. There are many diseases, however, which bear no relationship to the aging process as such, but older people succumb to them more readily simply because they have increasingly less resistance to disease in general.

In practice, diseases in old age fall into two broad groups: those which are common only in the elderly, such as Paget's disease, Parkinsonism, stroke, metabolic bone disease and some cancers; and those which occur in youth, middle or old age but present unusual features in the elderly. In this second and much larger group, classic symptoms are often replaced in old people (as mentioned for pneumonia) by one or more vague indicators that all is not well. These include disinclination to eat or

drink, weight loss, dizziness, confusion, incontinence and a general failure to thrive. It is in interpreting these non-specific signals, and discerning and treating the underlying disorder, that the geriatrician's skill mainly lies.

In addition, old people are at risk from various events and conditions to which they have become liable because of failing faculties and general loss of function. Falls, the principal accident menace of later life, are a case in point. Repeated surveys in the United States and Britain have shown that well over one-third of the over-sixty-fives fall at least once a year, and the risk of falling increases markedly with advancing age; women are almost twice as vulnerable as men. Mostly there are no serious consequences, although — partly because old bones are somewhat brittle — fractures result in a small proportion of cases. The incidence of fractured hips, for instance — trivial in younger age groups — increases more than fivefold with great age.

The sheer predictability of the average geriatric fall — most occur in the home, in the course of some commonplace activity — underlines the fact

129

A loving embrace shared by an elderly couple reflects unique and special affection cultivated by their years together. Many couples can maintain the physical side of their relationship well into old age.

that it most often follows one or another of a number of predisposing factors. These include an increase in body "sway" in the elderly; diminished reflexes; perhaps general debility; and the use of some drugs, especially those prescribed for raised blood pressure. Only about one-quarter of falls are thought to be due to "drop attacks," sudden episodes in which the legs go unaccountably weak and the victim falls to the ground but does not lose consciousness. Drop attacks, which occur mainly in the very aged, are thought to be related to a fall in blood pressure or to a constriction of the blood supply to the brain caused by certain movements of the neck.

Hypothermia, a condition in which the body temperature drops dangerously low, is a more insidious hazard, and can strike in surroundings which are only mildly cool. If the deep temperature of the body falls below 95°F, the whole body is cold to the touch — even the abdomen and armpits — although the victim does not complain of feeling cold. Shivering, which is a defensive mechanism against cold, is reduced in the old and usually absent in this condition; instead, the body becomes markedly rigid. Movements and speech slow up, and vital functions become depressed. The victim becomes pale, confused, drowsy and finally loses consciousness. If no help is forthcoming, death is inevitable within a few hours. Again, the predisposing factors are intrinsic ones: the old are more susceptible to hypothermia than younger people because of their reduced mobility, impaired blood supply and the decreased insulating properties of their skin. For these reasons, it is imperative that the homes of elderly people should be adequately heated at all times.

Old people do not need to be wrapped in cotton in case they break. For the most part they compensate for functional and sensory deficit by taking life at a more leisurely pace and avoiding — or becoming extra attentive in — situations of potential hazard. But when they are ill or injured, it is imperative that they receive prompt and informed medical care. Admittedly, it is sometimes difficult even for the most enlightened physician to know at what point normal aging shades into a decline brought about by a disorder, or perhaps by self-neglect and depression. Yet the distinction is a

Alex Comfort

Champion of the Elderly

Dr. Alex Comfort is one of the world's foremost gerontologists —a specialist in the study of the processes involved in aging. Indeed, he may be said almost to have founded the study as a science, and to have brought considerably closer the time when some of those processes may come under human control.

Born in February 1920, in London, England, Comfort received his education at Trinity College, Cambridge, before qualifying in medicine at the London Hospital. Aged nineteen at the outbreak of World War II, he was a conscientious objector and it was during this period that he took to publishing poetry, some of which was politically aimed against the notion of an all-powerful central government, promoting instead Comfort's strong views on individual responsibility.

Following the war, Comfort involved himself in biological research, initially as a Nuffield Research Fellow and later at University College, London, as the head of a Medical Research Council. The first-ever recipient of a doctorate of science in gerontology from London University, he was the author of *The Biology of Senescence*, a work that became a standard textbook on the aging process.

In 1974 Comfort emigrated to the United States to take up a position as Fellow at the Institute for Higher Studies in Santa Barbara, Professor in the Department of Pathology at the University of California Medical School at Irvine, and lecturer in the Department of Psychiatry at Stanford University.

Comfort's main contention is that present-day society is far too quick to see senior citizens as physically or mentally infirm, slow in understanding, and tending to stick to rigid routines. He proposes a fight back on the part of the elderly against this determined role-imposition by society, a fight to show that at "retirement" age there is a wide range of rewarding options open to all who wish to remain alert and active. A major part of the modern syndrome of growing old, he says, is simply that people are obliged to act as if all they are able to do is to wait for kindly death to release them from being a burden to themselves and to others. Yet many of the world's greatest and most useful inventions and creative works have been produced by those aged more than sixty. The mental approach is a critical factor.

As a biologist, however, Comfort's research has been at least as thorough into the physical, somatic effects of aging. Much of the process is now understood; more understanding still may lead to the possibility of halting the process altogether—one of Comfort's acknowledged goals.

A writer of accomplishment, even apart from his poetry, Comfort has long been in demand as a documentary writer on several biologically-linked topics. One of his most famous books was *The Joy of Sex*, edited by him and first published in 1972. Although somewhat controversial, it became a bestseller and was followed by the even more outspoken *More Joy of Sex*.

With advancing age, the chemical composition of bone changes. The once tightly packed fibers (below) become less dense (bottom), causing osteoporosis, which increases the risk of bone breakage.

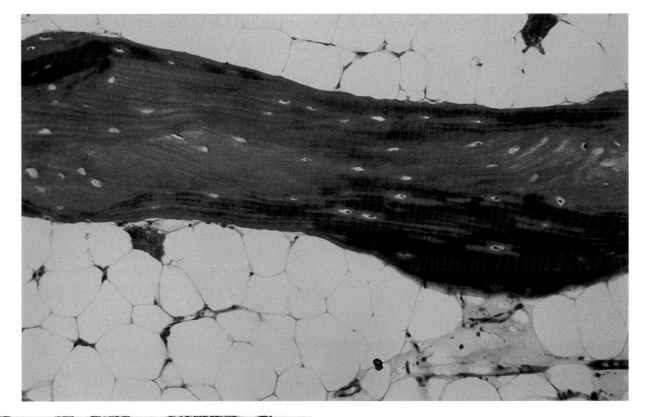

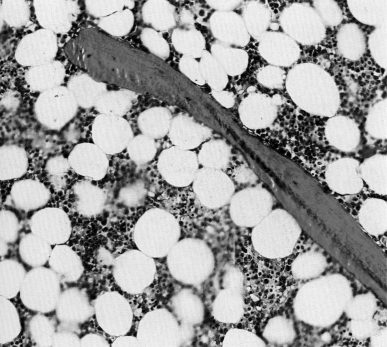

critical one, for illness or injury can be successfully treated—or at least greatly relieved—in old age.

Good Health and Long Life

One effect of gerontological advance has been to force a reappraisal of vigorous treatments in the elderly, including surgery, formerly performed more as a palliative rather than in the expectation of cure. It is now evident that, since surgical risk increases only gradually until the eightieth year, if dramatically thereafter, surgery is an increasingly attractive proposition for the older patient, in view of the long life expectancy of the aged population as a whole. A prime example is hip replacement for osteoarthritis, arguably the most successful procedure for alleviating one of the miseries of later life. Elderly patients are easier to anesthetize (if slower to come round) and are today less likely to be at risk from surgery itself. In geriatric medicine, then, it can be seen that the old may take longer to recover, but they do get better all the same. As one American wryly points out: "Surprising survival

and recovery is another characteristic of disease in old age."

Much more remarkable was the discovery, in a year-long study in Scotland, that the older severely debilitated hospital patients were, the longer they survived. The average length of stay in a hospital before death went from three months for those from sixty-five to seventy-four years of age, to six months for those aged seventy-five to eighty-four, and to seven months for men and an astounding thirteen months for women over the age of eighty-five. It can also be seen, therefore, that even the very old, who may have become saddened by disease and disability, can be treated and comforted so that they pass the time in contentment.

Yet disease and debility are not inevitable concomitants of old age. And, of course, it is never too late to correct some of the bad habits (such as poor nutrition, lack of exercise, smoking and heavy drinking) which are contributory factors in disease. Experiments have shown that a switch to a healthier life style can yield positive dividends even

in the over-seventies. In fact, in a study carried out for the American Administration on Aging some years ago, seventy-year-old men who joined a year-long exercise program emerged with the physical reactions of men thirty years younger.

Certainly normal aging involves decline in function, but this is gradual and its impact is cushioned by the decades over which it takes place. Abrupt decline is usually caused by illness, not age. For the most part, human beings live out their span on a vast functional reserve which is inherited in the genes and which is not significantly eroded until late old age. Meanwhile, because neither immortality nor rejuvenation are scientifically feasible, the main aim of gerontology is to find ways of postponing old age, and of providing remedies to diseases and disorders common at this stage of life. In other words, aging must still take place, but it could be made to happen later in life. This would give people more chance of living out their finite life span in tolerable conditions — extra years of vigor, instead of dependency.

Most commonly occurring in elderly people, a stoop is the result of a gradual shrinkage of the disks between the vertebrae of the spine. This causes curvature and loss of up to three inches in height.

Presbyopia (below) is an eyesight disorder common in people over sixty-five years of age. It is a condition in which the lens of the eye becomes stiff and enlarged, gradually reducing its ability to change shape to focus on nearby objects. Although there is no way to arrest the aging process of the eyes, the fitting of a suitable pair of eyeglasses (bottom right) may compensate more than adequately for failing sight.

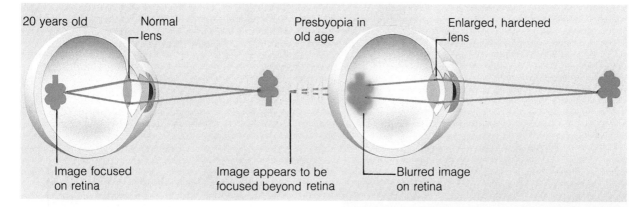

20 years old   Normal lens

Image focused on retina

Presbyopia in old age   Enlarged, hardened lens

Image appears to be focused beyond retina

Blurred image on retina

It is tantalizing to think that the rate — or rates — of aging could be changed. This has already been achieved, to some extent, by modifying caloric intake in laboratory mice — small animals with a conveniently brief life span. But human beings are altogether more complex, and a central problem in experimental biology is that the sort of work required on human aging would occupy an impossibly long time scale — more years than the investigators themselves could hope to live. Among many promising lines of inquiry is what the great nineteenth-century British naturalist Charles Darwin called the "feminine advantage," namely the inescapable fact that, on average, women live longer than men.

In the 1970s a panel of experts from the Rand Corporation made a number of predictions concerning developments in medicine over the next half century. Within the next few years, they said, we should have drugs or techniques to deal with the rejection problem in organ transplantation without leaving the patient so immunosuppressed that he or she is likely to succumb to the first passing germ; artificial organs made of plastic, and with electronic components, would be available by the 1990s; biochemicals to stimulate the growth of new limbs and organs would be developed by 2020; and the chemical control of aging would be possible by the year 2025.

Whether all this will come to pass remains to be seen — the first fully artificial heart, for instance, was implanted in a patient in 1984. What is certain, however, is that medical practice will change almost beyond recognition, for the future lies not so

135

The pituitary was once thought to be responsible for the reduction in function of other endocrine glands in old age. Recent studies have revealed no age differences in blood levels of pituitary hormones.

After retirement most elderly people channel their energies into new pastimes, often involving work in the community. Many participate in group activities, from fund-raising to political campaigns.

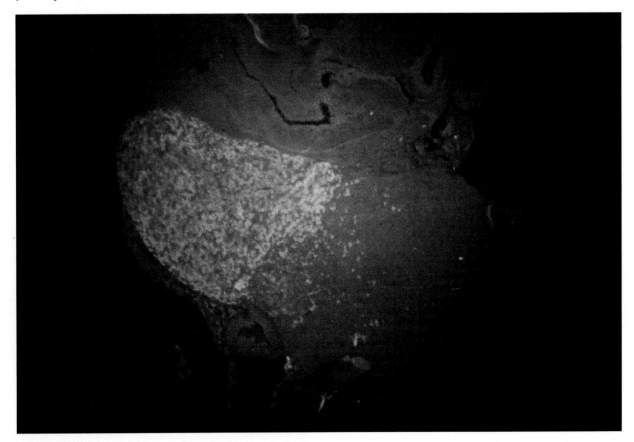

much in the pill and the potion, but more in direct intervention in the events of the cell. In fact, despite contemporary limitations on technique and application, cells themselves may even be removed from the body and, using the techniques of gene splicing, "reprogrammed" at the workbench before being replaced. At a more mundane level, however, it is also true to say that, as always, improved social welfare, public health measures and preventive medicine will do more to influence morbidity and mortality than all the hi-tech ever invented.

For the time being, however, longevity is a question of good luck, good genes—and perhaps something else? Centenarians, for instance, are people who seem almost to have outgrown mere old age — mostly still active and showing little evidence of the chronic disease and disability so often associated with great age. Moreover, they nearly always see themselves as being fit. It is interesting that everyone who has ever had much to do with a group of centenarians hints at some elusive psychological factor in their longevity — could it be sheer willpower? There are many wonderful old folk who remain so alert and vigorous that the rest of us pray that we shall be like them when we in our turn grow old.

The "Graying of Nations"

Western governments are today facing what is perhaps the biggest demographic challenge in history. More people are surviving into old age — and a ripe old age at that — than ever before. Already the over-sixty-fives account for 11 per cent of the population of the United States. But by the year 2025, when this "graying of nations" is expected to reach a peak, between one-sixth and one-quarter of the American population will be over sixty-five. By the same critical year, Britain and France will each be populated by 18.6 per cent old people, West Germany by 20 per cent, and Japan,

with an estimated minimum of 21.3 per cent, will have the highest proportion.

What is causing most concern is the fact that the increase is going to be most marked among the "grand elderly." In the United States, the number of over-eighty-fives will treble in the next half century. Even in a small country such as Belgium, where the number of over-eighties has already more than quadrupled since 1920, the grand elderly will increase by forty per cent by the turn of the century. France (which claims to have been the first "aged" country) was first to appoint a government minister for the aged with the declared intention of allowing them "the freedom to choose as long as possible their way of life and fulfill their existence with dignity." Three major factors have brought about this progressive graying of developed nations: a falling birthrate, the drop in the infant mortality rate fifty or more years ago, and increased life expectancy. The immense social, economic and

political implications of this trend were spelled out at the World Assembly on Aging held in 1982. It was generally agreed that, if the old are not to become an intolerable burden on a reduced working population, steps should be taken to offer them a new deal — and principally to help them to remain fit and well integrated in the community for as many as possible of their remaining years.

It was admitted that in the past there had been the tendency to proceed on the basis that everyone over the age of sixty has one foot in the grave — and to look no further than bundling them all into homes. The Canadians in particular conceded that their rate of institutionalization of the elderly had been wholly inappropriate. A more sophisticated approach to the needs of the elderly would take into account that most of them do not suffer from physical or mental decrepitude. As a leading British geriatrician, Professor Bernard Isaacs, has pointed out: "The numbers of old people who are not

incontinent, who have never had a stroke, a fall or a pressure sore, who are not housebound, chairbound or bedbound, run into millions."

The World Assembly generated a number of pious hopes with regard to mobilizing the elderly fit as a resource, making use of their unique fund of skills and experience in some productive way. But no government has yet come forward with a sufficiently flexible set of proposals, and it remains difficult to see how this utilization could be achieved (except perhaps in isolated instances) in a situation of persistent high unemployment for populations as a whole.

Meanwhile, many old people — no longer content to remain a passive lobby — are beginning to press their own claims. In the United States, for instance, today's old people — survivors of the 1930s depression and global war — are much more vocal politically than their contemporaries elsewhere. The American Association of Retired Persons has yielded a coalition of active workers,

called Gray Panthers, fighting for acknowledgment that "those of us over sixty-five are just like people under sixty-five. We have the same needs for housing, adequate medical care, financial security, sex. There's nothing different about us."

What these activists most want to change are the stereotypes of "agism," in which old age is seen as some kind of chronic illness — a rehearsal perhaps for death — and the aged themselves as slow-witted, unemployable, asexual and ill. Leading campaigner Alex Comfort made the point: "According to modern gerontology, some seventy-five per cent of what we now call 'old age', viewed as an accumulation of penalties and disabilities, is a product of institutions and of attitudes, not of biology."

Retirement by Obligation

A big stumbling block, of course, is the business of compulsory retirement. It can be seen as an extremely divisive practice in the light of the fact

On reaching formal retirement age, the elderly man (left), after ending his old career, commenced a new one. In Japan traditional concern for the elderly is often expressed in terms of retraining after retirement.

The Gray Panthers is a national organization that fights age discrimination. Among its aims is the elimination of mandatory retirement, and negative portrayals of older people by the media.

*Much of retirement is normally
spent in reasonably good health.
Individuals may wish to participate
in leisurely pursuits or attend classes
for general interest or personal
improvement.*

*The facial expression in Felix
Conrad's lithograph of a* Coalface
Worker *epitomizes the jaunty,
worldly-wise confidence that many
people attain in later adulthood —
experience that society can use.*

that people in positions of real power — states-men, for instance, and heads of industry — can hang on indefinitely, whereas most working people are obliged to step down at sixty or sixty-five. It is interesting that in a highly prosperous nation such as Japan, which has more of a tradition of working into old age (and where an unemployment level of two per cent is described as "relatively high"), the retirement age has been raised from fifty-five to sixty; workers reaching formal retirement are frequently reemployed by the same company. Many other countries, however, are looking for voluntary retirement in the fifties.

Until agism is conquered, many people will continue to enter retirement with the feeling that they have been made obsolete overnight. As Dr. Comfort says: "We make people socially old by retiring them. We may even, by the same token, make them physically old, for mind, body and society interact in a degree that can still amaze us." One way, perhaps, of gaining recognition for society's senior citizens would be to concede that, if it were not for the contribution of the recently retired in offering their services to hospitals, community support schemes and the like, the outlook for the underprivileged grand elderly in our society might be even bleaker than it already is.

The notion of formal retirement — as a well-earned rest for the mass of the working population — arose in the days when life expectancy was perhaps twenty or thirty years shorter than it is today. Now that there are moves to pull retirement age down into the fifties, most people have about one-quarter of the expected span still to live. It is important, therefore, to get away from Industrial Revolution notions of retirement as a sort of brief terminal interlude before death and to recognize that today's post-retirement phase represents a sizable volume of the milk of human experience which should not be allowed to go sour.

Primitive societies do not cast out their old folk; they make use of their abilities to the end. In Western society, largely obsessed with youth, it seems there is no percentage to be had from the fund of wisdom and experience which can be accumulated with age. Maggie Kuhn, founder of the Gray Panthers, recognized that old folk suffer more from frailty of status than of body or mind.

Appendix 1: Risk Factors in Prenatal Development

There are many factors in the environment that can compromise prenatal development. Some environmental hazards that affect the mother, or substances which she ingests, are relatively mild in their effects. Others, such as potent drugs, viruses or major radiation exposure, are teratogenic—that is, liable to cause major deformities in the embryo, even death. Development of the embryo is most likely to be disrupted during organogenesis (when organs are being formed), particularly between fifteen and sixty days after conception, at which time such influences commonly produce congenital malformations. Disturbances during the fetal period are usually less catastrophic, but still potentially threatening, especially to the developing brain and nervous system. Listed here are some of the agents and influences that are known to be harmful to an unborn child.

Alcohol Even modest drinking by the mother during pregnancy can endanger her unborn child, especially if she also suffers from malnutrition. Alcohol affects the fetal brain and possibly also the muscles, and many babies born to a mother with a drink problem are physically debilitated. Alcoholism affects up to two per cent of women of childbearing age. Excessive drinking results in fetal alcohol syndrome, characterized by stunted growth, mental retardation, possible congenital malformations (particularly of the face) and severe psychological problems. There is a ten per cent risk of fetal alcohol syndrome even when the mother takes only a couple of drinks a day, and the risk rises sharply with increasing consumption. One study has shown that the likelihood of a growth-retarded infant is doubled if the mother drinks or smokes during pregnancy; if she drinks *and* smokes, the risk is quadrupled. Smoking by itself during pregnancy may cause more harm to the fetus than drinking alcohol.

Anesthesia and Analgesia During labor, while the fetus is still linked to the mother's respiratory and circulatory systems, anesthetics and analgesics are sometimes given to ease pain. The analgesic most often used for this purpose is meperidine hydrochloride (Demerol); general anesthesia is usually withheld until delivery. These substances may cross the placental barrier and act as central nervous system depressants also on the fetus, making the baby liable to anoxia (oxygen starvation). Obstetricians have therefore to weigh the value of gaining relief for the mother against the possible risk to the fetus.

There is seemingly no threat to the fetus from betaendorphin, one of a group of "natural opiates" which is present at quite high levels in the bloodstreams of women just before childbirth.

Drugs Many drugs — even aspirin, the most commonly used medication during pregnancy — involve some element of risk to the fetus, and some are teratogenic. In this latter category are certain tranquilizers, antibiotics, anticonvulsants, antitumor agents and anticoagulants (although not heparin). Androgenic agents (synthetic hormones used to prevent miscarriage) may produce masculinization of female fetuses. The thalidomide tragedy of the late 1950s and early 1960s, which resulted in terrible deformities (although very few in the United States, where the drug was never approved for use), alerted doctors to the dangers of using drugs during pregnancy. Today prescribing is limited almost entirely to essential medications. Heroin is the most notorious among drugs of abuse. Babies born to heroin users are similarly addicted and withdrawal from heroin can be life-threatening in the newborn. Lysergic acid diethylamide (LSD) has been found to be teratogenic.

Heat Immersion of the mother's body in very hot water during pregnancy may raise the fetal temperature to a point which endangers the formation of the central nervous system. Women have given birth to malformed babies after having regularly relaxed in hot tubs and jacuzzi spas — normally heated to between 100°F and 106°F—for up to an hour.

Heavy Metals Lead and cadmium in drinking water from old water pipes, and various other heavy metals, can damage the fetus. Water from such pipes should be run off for a minute or two before use to flush away any residues.

 Malnourishment It is difficult to distinguish the effects of malnourishment from those of other aspects of social deprivation, but chronically underfed mothers are known to have babies of low birthweight. This is a threat to perinatal survival and a later development.

 Pathogens There are many disease agents which may endanger an unborn child who is, after all, wholly dependent on the well-being of the mother. Those most positively incriminated in the incidence of deformities in newborn babies are: the rubella (German measles) virus, cytomegalovirus, the *Herpes simplex* virus, the syphilis bacterium, and the parasite responsible for toxoplasmosis.

Rubella infection in the first trimester of pregnancy is catastrophic, causing damage such as cardiac anomalies, blindness, deafness and mental retardation in up to 20 per cent of infants born. The earlier the infection, the greater the risk to the embryo. Less severe damage may result from infections contracted later in pregnancy.

Cytomegalovirus, which is common in the United States, occurs in the female genital tract. Infection during the first trimester can be fatal to the embryo. Later infection may cause damage to the fetal brain and eyes.

The herpes virus attacks the fetus late in pregnancy, most often during delivery. It also causes damage to the central nervous system of the newborn baby, endangers eyesight, and can result in death.

Primary maternal syphilis (that is, syphilis acquired during pregnancy) almost invariably has an effect on the fetus unless treatment is given before the sixteenth week. Stillbirths result in one-quarter of untreated cases. Secondary syphilis (established before pregnancy begins) rarely affects the fetus.

Toxoplasmosis usually runs a mild course in adults, but the parasite — a single-celled protozoan occasionally found in contaminated meat — crosses the placenta, causing retardation, blindness or deafness in the fetus.

 Radiation High doses of radiation are extremely teratogenic; dangerous radiation includes hard X rays, gamma rays and the radiation emitted by radioactive substances. Termination of pregnancy may be recommended when exposure has exceeded 25,000 millirads. Although caution is advised with X rays or diagnostic tests using radioisotopes on pregnant women, the amount of radiation involved is usually quite low, and radiologists are well aware of the risks. However, the effect on the fetus of prolonged exposure to sources of low-level radiation, such as that from television screens and visual display units (VDUs), is now causing concern.

 Smoking Evidence of the potential harm of smoking during pregnancy has been mounting for half a century. Damage is caused by raised carbon monoxide levels (and consequent shortage of oxygen) in the maternal blood supply, and by the effects of various chemicals in tobacco, especially nicotine. Smoking increases the risk of miscarriage, low birthweight and fatal birth defects; there is also an increased tendency to sudden infant death (crib death) among babies of women who smoke. Men who smoke generally have higher rates of infertility than nonsmokers.

 Spermicides Spermicidal agents — contraceptive jelly, foam or cream — are not infallible in preventing pregnancy and may cause harm if conception does take place. Women using spermicides at the time of conception appear to run more than twice the normal risk of birth defects; the rate of miscarriage is one-and-a-half times higher than normal.

 Stress It is difficult to isolate the effects of stress during pregnancy from those of other negative factors which may be present, particularly if the stress has a psychological origin. But it is known that maternal stress stimulates the secretion of the hormone epinephrine, and this causes constriction of capillaries and diverts the blood flow away to organs other than the womb. Prolonged stress could thus deprive the fetus of some of its oxygen, supplied by the mother's arterial blood via the placenta. Infants born to mothers prone to stress are more likely to show motor impairment of their nervous system in the immediate postnatal period.

Appendix 2: Milestones of Development

Birth to Age 1½

There exists no such creature as an average person, yet a "normal" person's "normality" is generally related to the average, in whatever context it is being considered. Normality thus relies on acceptable deviation from a measured average—and this in turn means that in the descriptions and statistics given here it is important to remember that people *are* different, but that if those differences exist within the acceptable limits of the average, then they are normal. In addition, aspects such as race, genetic background, social upbringing and overall care do have an inevitable effect upon people's bodies.

The information given is intended to provide a guide to average and normal aspects of life from birth to old age. Even then, any reader who finds his or her personal life history does not accord with the stated "norm" may consider it a consolation that he or she is in some way exceptional.

Hearing

At birth, hearing is a baby's most immediate sense, partly because it is one of the few senses actually usable in the womb. But although hearing may be acute, a visible response to noise is made only to sounds that are loud or sudden. Even at the age of four months, when there may be some attempt to aid identification of noise sources visually, actual response may be little more than a sideways turn of the head. By five or six

In the first seconds of life, each newborn is subjected to a series of tests in which he or she is assigned a score out of a total of ten points. A score of less than six in the tests indicates a potential need for medical treatment. The tests are for heart rate, respiration, muscle tone, skin color and reflexes; the series is named after the physician who introduced it in 1952, the American pediatrician Dr. Virginia Apgar.

Steps Toward Walking

Age in months		
	2	Can lift head when lying on stomach; but head droops forward when baby is sat up.
	4	Head erect when baby is sat up; can look around; legs can take own weight briefly when baby held in standing position.
	6	Can stand, supported, for a short time; mobility increased by learning to roll.
	8	Can stand, holding support; begins to crawl.
	10	Can walk when supported by hands only; can walk holding on to furniture.
	12	Can stand unsupported, briefly; can crawl up stairs.
	14	Can walk between supports; many falls.
	16	True walking begins.

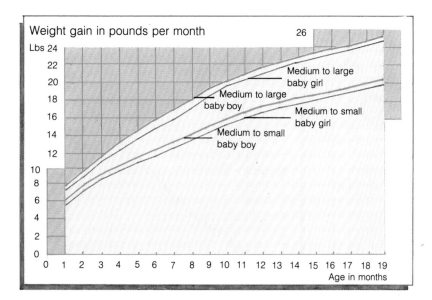

Weight gain in pounds per month

Lbs 24
22
20
18
16
14
12
10
8
6
4
2
0

26

Medium to large baby girl

Medium to large baby boy

Medium to small baby girl

Medium to small baby boy

0 1 2 3 4 5 6 7 8 9 10 11 12 13 14 15 16 17 18 19
Age in months

It is quite normal in the first week of life for a baby actually to lose weight —usually a few ounces only. Thereafter, a gain of some 5 to 7 ounces per week is normal for the first thirteen weeks, followed by a more gradual weight gain. A newborn requires 2½ to 3 ounces of milk daily for each pound of body weight. It is recommended that solid food be supplied only after the baby weighs at least 10 pounds or has reached the age of three months. At eighteen months, the "average" baby weighs 25 pounds.

months, however, such turning of the head is normal. Three-dimensional hearing, involving identification of sounds from above and below, is generally not achieved until between nine and twelve months of age.

Coordination

At birth, coordination is almost nonexistent. The normal reflexes—sucking, grasping and rooting—actually mask the otherwise helpless nature of a newborn. Even so, neonates do exhibit individual traits: they may spend long periods asleep or remain for long periods peaceably (or otherwise) awake; they may cry or gurgle, or stay relatively quiescent. But they are learning all the time, principally aurally.

Sleep Requirements

A newborn requires about twenty hours of sleep a day.

Thereafter, the average baby sleeps one hour less per day per month for the first four months. The pattern then tends to level out so that by the age of six months the average

daily sleep requirement is for about 15½ hours, remaining at that until at least the first birthday, by which time an interest in *not* sleeping is beginning to make itself felt.

Visual Progress

Age in months		
	1	Eyes fix on mother's face.
	2	Eyes begin to follow slow-moving objects.
	3	Beginnings of focusing; the environment takes on a three-dimensional appearance.
	4	Baby moves head to assist in vision.
	5	Baby actively inspects and searches.
	6	Eyes used for baby's own purposes, for example to locate objects to touch or hold.
	9	Beginnings of true concentration.
	12	Shows interest in two-dimensional shapes.
	15	Recognizes simple two-dimensional pictures.
	18	Begins to acknowledge concept of distance.

Age 1½ to 12

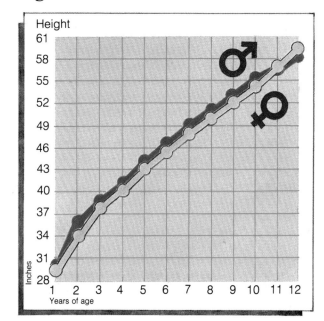

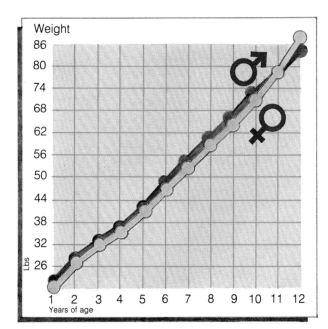

Physical Growth

At eighteen months, physical development in boys and girls is simultaneous, but by the time they are twelve, girls have taken the lead. By their second birthday, both boys and girls reach half of what will be their adult height—boys slightly in advance of girls. From then until the age of four, girls grow in height at a faster rate than do boys, and by the age of five their skeletal growth is distinctly—if slightly—ahead of the boys'. At the age of four the brain of both boys and girls has reached about three-quarters of its adult weight.

Between the ages of five and nine boys consistently grow more in each year than do the girls, despite natural fluctuations in the actual gains achieved (see diagram). From the age of ten, girls enter upon their "growth spurt," during which they may overtake the height of male classmates. There is not really a corresponding "weight spurt." The rate of weight increase continues in a smooth mathematical curve (as is evident on the chart above). All the same, it is at this age that girls tend briefly to overtake their male contemporaries in weight too, because boys seem to fall behind in the weight race for a year.

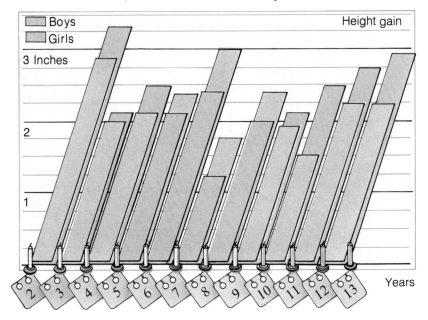

146

Ossification

The growing bones of children in this age group contain far more cartilage (gristle) than those of adults. Some—particularly those in the wrists—do not harden into bone (ossify) until around the time of puberty. Even the bones of the skull are not ossified until about eighteen months after birth.

But because cartilaginous "bones" are more flexible, less brittle, than true bones, they are less liable to fractures (and are faster in mending if fractures of the type classic for this age group—greenstick fractures—do occur.)

Teeth

At the beginning of this period the deciduous (milk) teeth canines are usually erupting, to be followed in about six months by the back molars. Thereafter, child and parents should be free of all teething problems save any caused by decay until the child nears the sixth birthday, when the permanent teeth begin to erupt, forcing out the milk teeth as they do so.

As with other aspects of growth, there are apparent similarities between boys and girls in the general order in which the teeth erupt. Yet there are also differences: teeth in girls almost all erupt up to seven months earlier than in boys—and lower canines erupt up to eleven months earlier.

(Third molars—the so-called wisdom teeth—erupt well after this age group; some never appear at all.)

In general, the permanent teeth grow into their new positions with little trouble. Some children, however, experience "crowding" of the teeth in the mouth. If this occurs, corrective and remedial treatment—perhaps the temporary fitting of a metal brace—can usually be arranged by an orthodontist.

Mental Development

Age in years		
	2	Self-oriented; beginnings of a distinction between "good" and "bad" as defined by parents.
	3	Beginnings of classification of things seen into types of object; expressions of frustration indicate growing independence and determination.
	4	Growing sense of subtlety: can be devious in trying to obtain desires; can comprehend environmental changes (although not their causes).
	5	Beginnings of sensitivity toward others and their wishes or feelings.
	6–8	An appreciation of time; self-image is explored as sense of morality grows.
	9	Classification and arrangement skills develop; use of speech takes over some previously demonstrative behavior.
	10–11	Need for approval often more important than own intentions; sense of sharing develops.
	12	Periods of reserved behavior alternate with gregarious boisterousness. Introspective self-exploration begins; some sexual feelings develop.

From early on, vision is a primary sense. The combination of the uses of vision for concentration on specific characteristics of objects and for coordination of physical movements is illustrated by the gradual improvement in drawing skills children exhibit at various ages.

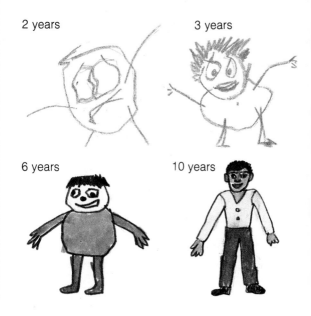

2 years   3 years

6 years   10 years

Age 12 to Adulthood

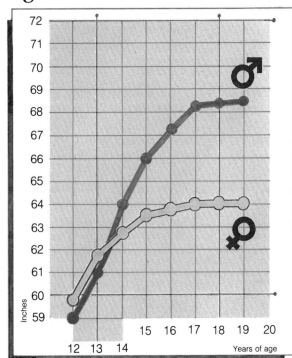

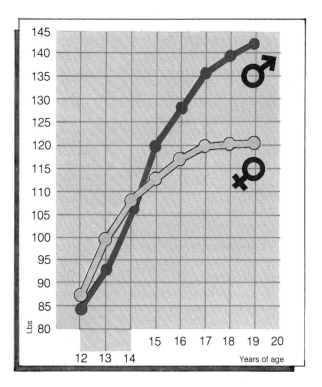

Girls: Height and Weight

At age twelve a girl's growth spurt is almost over: from now on the accent is on increasing body weight—which each girl does proportionately more than the boys of her age. The growth spurt is followed by the inevitable and natural increase in weight.

Boys: Height and Weight

At age twelve, the average boy weighs about 84½ pounds and is about 59 inches tall—which makes him three pounds lighter and nearly an inch shorter than the average girl of that age. But within two years it is time for the boys' growth spurt: statistically some seven inches in four years from the age of thirteen. Weight is augmented accordingly.

Girls: Puberty

Like boys, girls may suffer greatly from the skin condition acne throughout adolescence. Both sexes develop pubic hair and hair in the armpits. In women, the hips enlarge. The breasts develop from about the age of twelve; the area round the nipples also increases in pigmentation.

Slight vaginal secretion is normal before the onset of menstruation which, when it happens, is the real indication that a girl is becoming a woman. At this stage, although girls may be ready for motherhood in physical terms, few are emotionally prepared for it. The orange bars on the diagram (*above*) show the range of ages within which each "event" in puberty may begin

and end. The dark orange bands indicate the average age for the occurrence of each event.

Boys: Puberty

Although the physical changes that occur to make boys men do not appear so far-reaching or complex as those that turn girls into women, their significance to the individual is enormous. In the few cases in which those changes never occur emotional torment is the result.

The "breaking" of the voice is the most normally obvious outward sign of impending maturity and occurs between the ages of thirteen and seventeen. Other, more private, changes also take place. There is an increase in

148

the overall size of the scrotum and penis, around which pubic hair now grows. Spontaneous erections, which may have occurred for some years previously, are now linked to genuine sexual arousal. Facial hair appears.

Apart from these examples of the actions of male hormones, one in every ten boys also suffers from temporary breast development.

The purple bars on the diagram (right) show the range of ages within which each "event" in puberty may begin and end. The dark purple band indicates the average age for the occurrence of each event.

Metabolism in Later Life

Both men and women experience a considerable rise in blood pressure during the years in which they mature into adults. Between the ages of ten and twenty, for example, the blood pressure in men increases by thirty per cent, in women by twenty per cent. In both, blood pressure increases only very gradually after that until about the age of fifty. At that time, statistically just past the average for the menopause in women, women's blood pressure finally overtakes that of men, and continues to increase at a higher rate.

While blood pressure is increasing dramatically between the ages of ten and twenty, the pulse rate as measured during rest is actually decreasing almost as swiftly. From an average of around 66 heartbeats a minute

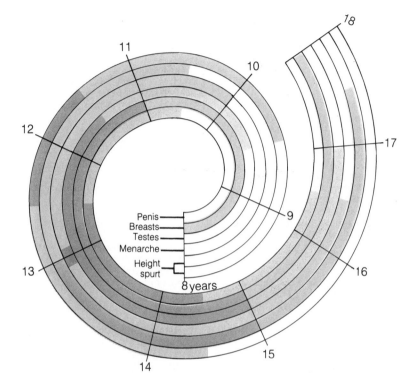

at age ten, by age twenty the average during rest is about 57 — more than thirteen per cent slower. And it continues to decrease until about age thirty, when the rate levels out at around 54 to the minute. Not until the mid-forties does the rate change again, after which there is a gradual increase for the following twenty-five years, so that by age sixty-five the average is around 70 heartbeats per minute while at rest.

In terms of purely physical strength, a woman is at her most powerful at about the age of eighteen, and although endurance wanes only slowly after then, actual strength decreases with some rapidity. Men are on average stronger than women (at a ratio, it has

been suggested, of 11:8), but they tend to peak in strength at the age of twenty-one. Although their power then declines with equal rapidity, men's average strength never decreases to women's greatest level — that is, giving men's peak strength a numerical value of 11, men's strength declines to about 9 by the age of seventy.

Western society encourages senescence through its insistence on retirement from daily work at the arbitrary age of sixty or sixty-five. Yet the fact remains that the basal metabolic rate — a measure of the speed at which the body "burns" its energy while at rest — declines at a ratio averaging only 38:35 between the ages of twenty and seventy.

Glossary

abortus an embryo that dies, most often because of an abnormality, and is expelled from the mother's uterus.

acne a skin complaint, most common during adolescence, in which inflammation of sebaceous glands leads to red pimples on the face and sometimes other areas.

amino acids a group of some twenty organic acids in the body which contain nitrogen and form the building blocks of protein molecules.

amniocentesis a diagnostic technique applied to pregnant women in which a small quantity of fluid is withdrawn from within the amnion through the abdominal wall by means of a fine tube. Some fetal abnormalities can be detected from the fluid or the cells it contains.

amnion the membranous, fluid-filled sac that surrounds a fetus as it develops within the uterus.

analgesia the relief of pain without a loss of consciousness.

androgenic promoting or producing masculine characteristics as, for example, do male sex hormones.

anencephaly a developmental abnormality of a fetus, in which the brain is lacking.

anesthesia the loss of sensation, including that of pain, in the whole or part of the body, especially as produced by anesthetic drugs.

anorexia nervosa a psychological condition found most commonly in adolescent girls, in which there is a refusal to eat adequately; it commonly leads to catastrophic weight loss and, in the worst cases, can result in death.

anoxia a lack of sufficient oxygen, particularly in the blood or in the supply to the tissues.

antibodies proteins formed in the body that are able to counteract the potential of foreign substances to harm the body; they are essential parts of the body's immune system.

antioxidants substances which "mop up" free radicals that attack the body tissues, believed by some to slow aging.

Apgar assessment a system of tests, named for its originator, Virginia Apgar, which are carried out on newborn babies to ascertain if functions such as heart rate, respiration and reflexes are normal.

asphyxia an inability to breathe caused by lack of oxygen in the air or blockage of the respiratory passages or lungs.

atheroma a thickening of the artery walls with fibrous or fatty tissue, often leading to circulatory disorders.

atrophy the wasting of a body, organ or cell.

aurally by means of the ears.

autoimmune disease a disease in which the immune system of the body becomes overactive and reacts against some of the body's own tissues.

axillary of or in the armpit.

beta-endorphin one of the endorphins, substances produced naturally by the body that are thought to act as painkillers by binding to the same receptor sites in the brain that are utilized by compounds such as morphine.

blastocyst a very early stage in the development of an embryo, at which it comprises an outer hollow sphere of cells and within it, on one side, a solid mass of cells.

blastomeres the apparently similar cells formed by the early cell divisions of an embryo.

brown fat a type of fat tissue that occurs especially in young mammals and in mammals that hibernate. It is used in the production of heat for temperature regulation.

Caesarean delivery the delivery of a baby by removal from the womb through an incision in the abdominal wall. It is used especially where a normal delivery (via the vagina) is impossible or poses risks.

calcification the deposition of calcium compounds within tissues, for example, the normal accumulation of calcium phosphate in bone or abnormally of calcium in scar tissue.

canines the pointed teeth at the front corners of the mouth, one on each side of both upper and lower jaws; they are so called because they are especially well developed in carnivores such as dogs.

cardiac of the heart.

cardiovascular disease disease which affects the heart or the blood flow through blood vessels.

catheter a flexible tube introduced into an enclosed space within the body, such as the bladder, designed to withdraw fluid from that space.

celiac disease a wasting disease usually of children, in which the body is unable to absorb fats and some vitamins from the intestines.

chorion the outer membrane that encloses within it the amnion and fetus in the uterus.

chorionic sac the space contained within the chorion.

chorionic villus one of the fingerlike outgrowths of the outer surface of the chorion.

cleavage the early stage of development during which a fertilized egg divides repeatedly to form a small ball of apparently similar cells.

climacteric the time of cessation of reproductive ability; the term may be applied to either sex, but a definite cessation can generally be recognized only in women, in whom it is marked by the menopause.

colostrum the "milk" secreted by the mother's breast for the first day or two after a birth. It has a different composition from the later, true milk, but is rich in proteins and antibodies.

conceptus the fertilized ovum as it develops during the first few days after conception.

congenital present at birth, as are some diseases and malformations.

contraindication a factor that indicates that a certain course of action should not be carried out, that a specific drug or therapy should not be administered.

150

deciduous falling off; the term often refers to the first, or "milk" set of teeth which are shed and eventually replaced by the permanent set of teeth.

diabetes mellitus a disorder in which the pancreas is deficient in the production of insulin, a hormone that controls the levels of blood sugar (glucose) in the body.

dilatation the widening or opening of an orifice or channel.

ectoderm the outermost of three recognizable layers of cells which develop in the embryo; from it develop the skin and the nervous system.

embryo the developing baby from the time of fertilization up until the time that organs begin to form, after which it is termed a fetus. In humans the embryonic stage lasts about eight weeks.

embryonic disk the disk shape assumed by an embryo during about the third week of development.

endocrine describes the ductless glands and other tissues that secrete hormones, which control many body processes.

endoderm the innermost of three recognizable layers of cells which develop in the embryo; from it develops the alimentary system.

endometrium the membrane which forms the lining of the uterus.

epinephrine a hormone produced by the medulla of the adrenal glands; its effects include an increased heart rate and blood supply to the muscles.

estrogen one of a group of hormones which give rise to female sexual characteristics and affect female reproductive activity.

extrauterine taking place outside the uterus, or womb.

Fallopian tubes the pair of tubes in the female abdomen which lead from close to each ovary into the uterus. The ovum released from an ovary travels along one of these tubes, and may be fertilized on its journey through it.

fetus the baby developing in the uterus from the time that organs begin to form until birth.

flora the varied collection of bacteria that are normal inhabitants of various parts of the body, such as the skin, mouth cavity or intestines.

fluoridation the addition of small quantities of fluoride compounds to drinking water to assist in the prevention of tooth decay.

follicle a small sac or cavity, such as the hair follicle from which a hair grows.

geriatrician a medical practitioner who specializes in the problems of old age and their treatment.

gerontology the study of the processes involved in aging.

grasp reflex a reflex present in a newborn baby but disappearing after a few weeks, by which the baby tightly grips an object placed in the palm.

gynecology the study of the structure, function and disorders of the female reproductive system.

HCG human chorionic gonadotropin.

hormones substances, sometimes likened to chemical messengers, produced by ductless glands and other tissues within the body and released into the bloodstream. They are thus able to affect the functioning of parts of the body distant from where they are secreted.

human chorionic gonadotropin (HGC) a hormone produced by the placenta that helps to maintain the corpus luteum functioning in the ovary.

hypertrophy the growth of a cell, tissue or organ beyond its normal size.

hypothermia a state in which the body ceases to maintain its normal constant temperature and becomes chilled. It is a particular hazard for the elderly, for whom it can be fatal in a few hours. It is also known as exposure.

immunity the ability to withstand infection from outside the body. In response to proteins of invading organisms, immunity may be conferred by antibodies manufactured in the body's lymphatic system, or by the administration of vaccines.

immunosuppression treatment with drugs that counteract the body's normal reaction to foreign tissue. Such drugs are administered, for instance, when transplants are undertaken, but have the disadvantage that they lower the body's resistance even to mild infections.

implantation important stage in the development of an embryo by which it fixes itself to the uterine wall; implantation is necessary before a placenta can be formed.

intrauterine within the uterus or womb.

intravenous feeding the passing of a solution of nutrients via a tube directly into a vein, rather than taking in food through the mouth.

IQ test a test that sets out to measure the intelligence of the person tested; IQ stands for Intelligence Quotient. Opinion is divided on how accurate such tests are, and what exactly is being measured.

jaundice a condition in which the skin and the white of the eyes are colored yellow, caused by an excess of bile pigments circulating in the blood, and often symptomatic of a liver disorder.

kinesthesia the perception by the brain of movements of the body and overall position, derived from sensors in muscles, joints and tendons.

lanugo fine downy hair which covers the fetus in the womb; it is shed before birth.

lymphatic system a system of glands and vessels which drain fluid from the tissues of the body together with dead cells and bacteria. The system returns the fluid, lymph, to veins in the neck region, after it has passed through the lymph nodes which act as cleansing filters.

malnutrition any condition resulting from eating a diet that does not include all the substances and factors necessary for a healthy life.

melanocytes cells that produce melanin, the skin pigment responsible for black and brown colors in skin and hair.

menarche the initial onset of a girl's menstruation.

menopause the final cessation of a woman's menstruation.

mesoderm the middle of three recognizable layers of cells which develop in the embryo; from it develop the heart and skeletal muscle, and the blood.

metabolism the biochemical processes, concerned with building up tissue or with breaking it down, that take place within each living organism.

metabolites substances that are the products of metabolism.

molars the grinding teeth at the rear of the jaw.

moniliasis a disorder caused by infection with the fungus *Monilia*.

mores the customary practices and moral code of a society or tribe.

morula an early embryo, when it consists only of a tiny ball of similar cells. It is in this stage that the embryo arrives at the uterus from a Fallopian tube.

myxedema a disease in which the thyroid gland secretes insufficient hormone. Symptoms include a low metabolic rate, thickening and drying of the skin, and hair loss.

neonate a newborn baby.

nerve fibers strands of nervous tissue along which are conducted the electrical impulses which convey sensory and other information from the body to the central nervous system and motor impulses from the central nervous system to the body.

neurological of the structure, function or disorders of the nervous system.

notochord a stiff rod which forms the "backbone" of the most primitive vertebrates. In higher vertebrates, including humans, a notochord is

present for a short time in the early embryo. The elements of the true spine form around it.

obstetrician a medical practitioner who specializes in dealing with pregnancy and associated problems.

opiate a drug derived from opium, or a synthetic alternative, that induces sleep and dulls pain.

organogenesis the process of formation of recognizable organs and tissue types in an embryo. It marks the transition from the embryo stage to that of the fetus.

orthodontist a dental practitioner whose main concern is with correction of malformations or faulty growth of the teeth.

ossification the formation of bone, particularly the formation of hard bone from its softer forerunner, cartilage.

osteoarthritis a disorder of the joints in which the cartilages at the joint and the nearby bone are gradually worn away.

osteoporosis a disorder in which the bones are progressively weakened by loss of calcium, leaving a rather porous structure.

ovulation the shedding of a mature egg (ovum) from the ovary.

oxytocin a hormone produced in the posterior part of the pituitary gland. It stimulates contractions of the uterus during labor and promotes the release of milk from the breasts.

Paget's disease a disorder in which the bones tend to progressively enlarge and soften; the skull and legs may be particularly affected.

pancreas a large digestive gland which opens into the small intestine and contains tissue which produces the hormone insulin, important in the regulation of blood sugar.

Parkinsonism a group of nerve disorders in which the patient shows abnormally decreased mobility, rigidity in the muscles, and tremors.

parotid one of the salivary glands situated at the angle of the lower jaw.

parotitis inflammation of the parotid gland, as occurs in mumps.

parturition the process of giving birth.

patency in the state of being patent— that is, open or spread wide.

pedagogics the science of teaching.

pediatric of the treatment of children's disorders.

pediatrician a medical practitioner who specializes in the treatment of the disorders of children.

pelvis the hip region, enclosed by the three bones of the pelvic girdle on each side plus the sacrum and coccyx of the lower spine. The renal pelvis is the funnel-shaped top of the ureter which collects urine from the calyx of each kidney.

perinatal around the time of birth.

phimosis a condition in which the tightness of the foreskin makes it impossible to draw it back over the head of the penis.

phonetic of symbols that consistently represent the sounds of speech; few languages have a written form that is truly phonetic.

pinworm a type of parasitic worm about one-third of an inch long which can infest the lower part of the intestine in humans; more often found in children than adults, it causes irritation near the anus by emerging at night to lay eggs.

placenta a spongy structure with many blood vessels that forms in the uterus during pregnancy. Within it, maternal and fetal blood circulations lie close together, and respiratory and nutritional exchange take place between them. In the third stage of labor, the placenta is expelled as the afterbirth.

premenstrual occurring before a menstrual period.

premolars chewing teeth at the side of the mouth between canines at the front and the true molars at the rear. The premolars are present in both milk and adult sets of teeth.

presenting symptom the symptom of a disorder that is noticed by a patient or brought to the attention of a physician. In disorders that have a number of symptoms or side effects, it is not necessarily the most important effect or symptom of the disease, and can vary between age groups or individuals.

primordium the earliest rudiment of a structure or organ that is recognizable in the course of development.

progeria premature development in young people of symptoms of old age, such as falling hair, wrinkled skin and generally senile appearance; it is sometimes associated with a defective pituitary gland.

prognosis the forecast by medical opinion of the probable course of a disorder in a patient, and the prospects for recovery.

prostaglandins chemicals of a hormonal type manufactured by the body. First isolated from prostate gland extract (hence their name), they occur in many parts of the human body and are significant in several reactions, including the dilation of the neck of the uterus during childbirth.

psychotherapy the treatment of a disorder by psychological factors rather than by drugs or surgery.

puberty the age at which an individual becomes capable of sexual reproduction.

pyloric stenosis the narrowing of the intestinal passage caused by abnormal thickening of the intestinal wall in the region of the pylorus—at the exit of the stomach where the stomach opens to the small intestine.

reflexes built-in patterns of human behavior that appear in response to a particular stimulus, physical or emotional.

renal of the kidney.

scrotum the external muscular sac surrounding the testes.

seborrheic dermatitis a disorder of the skin in which there is overactivity of the skin grease glands (sebaceous glands) associated with reddish inflamed skin covered with greasy scales or dandruff.

sebum the fatty secretion produced by the skin's sebaceous glands.

senescence the aging of an organism, particularly that period when its powers are in noticeable decline.

somatotropin growth hormone.

somites the divisions, or segments, apparent in all vertebrate embryos—including those of humans—as they develop.

sperm count a measure of the number of live, mobile sperms in a sample of semen, which provides a useful indication of potential fertility.

spleen an organ situated in the abdominal cavity near the liver; it contains many blood vessels and is one site of the breakdown of the body's red blood cells.

startle reflex a series of movements produced by a baby in response to loud noises, sudden movements, and other sudden stimuli.

stepping reflex a reflex, present in young babies but later lost, consisting of stepping movements in response to being touched on the sole of the foot.

subcutaneous just beneath the skin.

sucking reflex a reflex, present in young babies, who suck at a nipple or any similar-shaped object placed against the lips.

surfactant a "wetting" agent that reduces the surface tension of a substance.

teratogens literally monster-producers; substances or agents, such as radiation, that can cause damage to an unborn child.

testosterone a hormone that causes the body to develop male secondary sexual characteristics, such as a deep voice and facial hair, and is necessary for proper functioning of the male sex organs.

thermoregulation the processes by which body temperature is regulated and kept at a constant level.

threadworm pinworm.

toxoplasmosis a disease caused by a protozoan parasite; its most devastating effects are caused on young babies and fetuses in the womb, when it can cause brain damage, blindness, deafness or even intrauterine death.

trauma an injury to the body caused by external violence; the term is also used in psychiatry to denote a massive emotional shock.

trimester one-third of the nine-month period of pregnancy.

ultrasound sound pitched above the frequency limit of human hearing that can be used to provide an electronic image of some of the internal organs of the body, a technique called sonography.

urticaria an itchy condition of the skin, often accompanied by swelling. It can occur as an allergic reaction to certain foods or drugs, in which the skin comes up in whitish weals.

uterus the womb, the part of the female reproductive tract in which a fetus develops.

vaccination originally describing immunization against smallpox, the term now means any process by which a person is rendered immune to a specific disease, involving the injection (or other means of introducing to the bloodstream) of a vaccine of dead or weakened pathogens to cause the natural production of antibodies, which can then act to neutralize the disease.

ventilation the movement of air in and out of the lungs.

vernix caseosa a coating of a waxy secretion and dead epidermal cells that covers the fetal skin during the final three months before birth.

voluntary neural pathways the nervous connections whose functions are under the control of the will, rather than being automatic.

Werner's syndrome progeria.

wet nurse a woman who is employed to suckle the child of another woman.

Illustration Credits

A Lifetime of Development
6, Bull Publishing Consultants/Nick Birch.

Life Before Birth
8, Illustration to *The Ruba'iyat of Omar Khayyam* by Rene Bull/Hodder and Stoughton, British Library/Bridgeman Art Library. 10, Biophoto Associates. 11, David Schaft/Science Photo Library. 12 (left) Omikron/Science Photo Library. 12 (right) and 13 (left) Dr. G. Schatten/ Science Photo Library. 13 (right) Dr. L. M. Beidler/Science Photo Library. 14, Sally and Richard Greenhill. 15 (left) Zefa. 15 (right) Zefa. 16, **Mick Gillah**. 17 (left) **Mick Saunders**. 17 (right) Science Photo Library. 18, Bull Publishing Consultants/ Nick Birch. 19, *Saskia as Flora* by Rembrandt/The Hermitage, Leningrad/ Bridgeman Art Library. 20, Clive Sawyer/ Zefa. 21, Nancy Durrell McKenna/ Camerapix Hutchison. 22, Nobelstiften Sweden. 23, Anthea Sieveking/Vision International. 24, Camerapix Hutchison. 25, Dr. C. Lightdale/Science Photo Library. 26, Sally and Richard Greenhill. 27 (left) Sally and Richard Greenhill. 27 (right) Syndication International. 28, Imagebank. 29, **Norman Swift**.

Studying Growth
30, Brian Moser/Camerapix Hutchison. 32, *Birth of the Virgin* by The School of the Veneto/Christie's, London/Bridgeman Art Library. 33, *Massacre of the Innocents* by Pieter Breughel/Kunsthistorisches Museum, Vienna/Bridgeman Art Library. 34, Mary Evans Picture Library. 35, *The Pinch of Poverty* by T. B. Kennington/ Coram Foundation, London/Bridgeman Art Library. 36, Mansell Collection. 37, *Fairies in a Nest* by John Austen Fitzgerald/Maas Gallery, London/ Bridgeman Art Library. 38, *Foundling Girls in the Chapel* by Sophie Anderson/Coram Foundation, London/Bridgeman Art Library. 39, Mary Evans Picture Library. 40, *The Young Seamstresses* by Alexis Harlamoff/Christie's, London/Bridgeman Art Library. 41, Mansell Collection. 42, *Virgin with Garland of Flowers* by Rubens/ Alte Pinakothek, Munich/Bridgeman Art Library. 43 (top) Sally and Richard Greenhill. 42 (bottom) Mansell Collection. 44, *Breakfast Under the Big Birch* by Carl Larsson/National Museum, Stockholm/ Bridgeman Art Library. 45 (left) Mansell Collection. 45 (right) Mary Evans Picture Library. 46 (left) H. Murray-Gritscher/ Zefa. 46 (right) and 47, *Venice*, by John Strickland Goodall/Christopher Wood Gallery/Bridgeman Art Library. 48, Kobal Collection. Foldout (outer) Courtesy of the Trustees of the British Library. (inner), **Mick Gillah, Norman Swift,**

Mick Saunders. 49, Douglas Dickins. 50, Mrs Björn Soldan/Oxford University Press. 51 (left) Sporting Pictures Ltd. 51 (right) Kobal Collection.

First Encounters
52, Bull Publishing Consultants/Nick Birch. 54, Leidmann/Zefa. 55 (left) Rex Features. 55 (right) *Julie and Louise* by William Lee-Hankey/Trustees of the Royal Society of Painters in Watercolours/ Bridgeman Art Library. 56 (top) Photri/ Zefa. 56 (bottom) Sally and Richard Greenhill. 57, Mary Evans Picture Library. 58, **Mick Gillah**. 59 (top) Bull Publishing Consultants/Nick Birch. 59 (bottom) David Hartley/Rex Features. 60, **Mick Saunders**. 61, Mary Evans Picture Library. 62 (left) Sally and Richard Greenhill. 62 (right) **Mick Gillah**. 63, Sally and Richard Greenhill. 64 (left) Rex Features. 64 (right) Imagebank. 65, **Mick Saunders**. 66, Bull Publishing Consultants/Nick Birch. 67, Sally and Richard Greenhill. 68, Rex Features. 69, Popperfoto. 70 (left) Sally and Richard Greenhill. 70 (right) Nancy Brown/ Imagebank. 71, Wendy Allen.

Preschool to Puberty
72, *The Kite* by Edward Wiethase/ Whitford and Hughes/Bridgeman Art Library. 74, Rex Features. 75 (top) **Norman Swift**. 75 (bottom) Sally and Richard Greenhill. 76, **Mick Gillah**. 77 (left) T. E. Thompson/BRI/Science Photo Library. 77 (right) Science Source/Science Photo Library. 78, Michael McIntyre/ Camerapix Hutchison. 79 (left) Sally and Richard Greenhill. 79 (right) Camerapix Hutchison. 80, **Mick Gillah**. 81, Benser/ Zefa. 82, Courtesy of the Trustees of the British Museum. 83 (top) *Children's Games* by Pieter Breughel/Kunsthistorisches Museum, Vienna/Bridgeman Art Library. 83 (bottom) A. Howland/Camerapix Hutchison. 84, Sally and Richard Greenhill. 85 (top) *Snap the Whip* by Winslow Homer/Butler Institute of American Art, Ohio. 85 (bottom) Ted McCausland. 86, Maria Montessori Training Centre. 87, Mary Evans Picture Library. 88, Sally and Richard Greenhill. 89, *Children Playing at Coach and Horse*/Roy Miles Gallery/Bridgeman Art Library. 90, Camerapix Hutchison. 93, Biophoto Associates. 94, Sally and Richard Greenhill. 95, Biophoto Associates.

The Turbulent Teens
96, *Bike – The Pure Dynamite Motorcycle Magazine*/Private Collection/Bridgeman Art Library. 98 (top) Camerapix Hutchison. 98 (bottom) Sarah Errington/ Camerapix Hutchison. 99, **Mick Saunders**. 100, **Mick Saunders**. 101, **Mick**

Saunders. 102, Sally and Richard Greenhill. 103, Sally and Richard Greenhill. 104, Bernard Regent/ Camerapix Hutchison. 105, A. Hubrich/ Zefa. 106, Nick Hadfield/Camerapix Hutchison. 107 (left) Liba Taylor/ Camerapix Hutchison. 107 (right) Ron Reike/Zefa. 108/109 (top) Henry Chalfant. 109 (bottom) Kobal Collection. 110, Sally and Richard Greenhill. 111 (top) Voigt/ Zefa. 111, (bottom) Yellowhammer, London for COI/DHSS.

The Road to Maturity
112, *The Gentle Art of Snowballing* by W. Heath Robinson/Private Collection/ Bridgeman Art Library. 114, Canadian Mining Corporation. 115, Tony Stone Worldwide. 116, Blume/Zefa. 117, Art Directors Photo Library. 118, Zefa. 119, Alexandre/Zefa. 120 (left) Biophoto Associates. 120 (right) Biophoto Associates. 121, Bramaz/Zefa. 122, Sally and Richard Greenhill. 123 (top) **Mick Gillah**. 123 (bottom) Biophoto Associates. 124 (top) ICI, London. 124 (bottom) Wendler/Imagebank. 125, **Mick Gillah**. 125 (inset) Mareshal/Imagebank. 126 (left) Novosti. 126 (right) Kobal Collection. 127, **Norman Swift**. 128, **Norman Swift**. 129, Tony Stone/Worldwide. 130, Zarember/ Imagebank. 131, Mitchell Beazley Publishers. 132 (top) Dr. Bryan Eyden/ Science Photo Library. 132 (bottom) Biophoto Associates. 133, Marron/Zefa. 134, Carlos Guarita/Reflex. 135 (top) **Mick Gillah**. 135 (bottom) *A Portrait of the Artist's Mother* by Rembrandt/Wilton House/Bridgeman Art Library. 136, Biophoto Associates. 137, AARP. 138, AARP. 139, Gray Panthers. 140, AARP. 141, *Kohlengarbeiter* by Conrad Felixmuller/Christie's, London/Bridgeman Art Library.

Appendixes
142, **Mick Saunders**. 143, **Mick Saunders**. 144, John Watney Photo Library. 145, **Norman Swift**. 146 (top) **Norman Swift**. 146 (bottom) **Mick Saunders**. 147, **Mick Saunders**. 148, **Norman Swift**. 149, **Mick Saunders**.

Index